YOUR
TURN

YOUR TURN

CAREERS, KIDS, AND COMEBACKS—
A WORKING MOTHER'S GUIDE

JENNIFER GEFSKY & STACEY DELO

with Kathleen Harris

HARPER
BUSINESS

An Imprint of HarperCollins*Publishers*

HarperCollins books may be purchased for educational, business, or sales promotional use. For information, please email the Special Markets Department at SPsales@harpercollins.com.

FIRST EDITION

Designed by Bonni Leon-Berman

Library of Congress Cataloging-in-Publication Data

Names: Gefsky, Jennifer, author. | Delo, Stacey, author.
Title: Your turn : career, kids, and comebacks—a working mother's guide / Jennifer Gefsky and Stacey Delo, with Kathleen Harris.
Description: First edition. | New York : HarperBusiness, [2019] | Includes bibliographical references and index.
Identifiers: LCCN 2019028491 (print) | LCCN 2019028492 (ebook) | ISBN 9780062893697 (hardcover) | ISBN 9780062893703 (ebook)
Subjects: LCSH: Working mothers. | Women—Employment re-entry. | Work and family. | Career development.
Classification: LCC HD6055 .G39 2019 (print) | LCC HD6055 (ebook) | DDC 650.1082—dc23
LC record available at https://lccn.loc.gov/2019028491
LC ebook record available at https://lccn.loc.gov/2019028492

---

19 20 21 22 23   LSC   10 9 8 7 6 5 4 3 2 1

JEN
For David, Grace, Henry, and Blake

STACEY
For Gabe, Rory & Toby

JEN + STACEY
For all the women out there navigating career + parenting.
We see you.

CONTENTS

YOUR
TURN

INTRODUCTION

Meet Jen

I never thought I would quit my job.

I grew up definitively middle class in Toledo, Ohio. It was not an ideal childhood, with an alcoholic father who was out of my life by the time I was twelve, offering no child support. Thankfully, my mom was an emergency room nurse and was able to provide enough to give my sister and me a stable home, although it wasn't always easy. I learned at an early age that financial security was everything. By the time I was about ten years old, the seed of ambition was planted. I knew I wanted to be able to support myself, and never have to rely on someone else to provide for me. I never wanted to be financially *stuck*. The struggles I saw my mom endure were not going to happen to me. So I became a worker bee at age eleven, over time holding almost every type of job imaginable: babysitting, ironing neighbors' shirts, working at McDonald's, valet parking, waiting tables, serving cocktails, working at the mall, and as a hospital emergency room clerk. I worked and paid my way through college and law school, and was happy to do so.

Thankfully, my determination paid off. I graduated from law school and moved to New York City at the age of twenty-six. I was recruited by a big, fancy law firm and made more money as a first-year associate than my parents ever made. I married my law-school sweetheart, David. My career really started humming and I was recruited to work at Major League Baseball four years later. At the age of thirty, I was selected by *Crain's New York* as a 40 under 40 Rising Star in New York City. Me?! A rising star in New York City? I felt practically invincible. Everything was going according to my plan.

I didn't stop there. Like many young, driven, successful women, I wanted it all: I wanted kids and I wanted my career. After seven years of hard-charging ladder climbing post–law school, it was time to start a family. I honestly did not think having kids would affect my career in a meaningful way. Looking back, I laugh at my own naivete.

Because then I actually had kids.

I returned to work full-time ten weeks after having my first child, and I didn't really lose my stride. Skip ahead thirteen months and I was pregnant again. This time my pregnancy and maternity leave were tougher. I also had a more senior and demanding position at Major League Baseball. My schedule was untenable: I woke up with the baby at 4 a.m., was out the door for work by 6:30 a.m., and was in the office by 8 a.m. with a full day of stressful work ahead of me. Cue the eye-rolls from colleagues when I ran to catch the 5:45 p.m. train to relieve the babysitter by 7:00. By the time I crashed into bed each night I was mentally and physically exhausted.

Why couldn't I handle this? What was I doing wrong? I felt I was failing in every aspect of my life—tired at home and just getting by at work. It wasn't a viable situation. So, twelve years into my career, I did the thing that I never thought I would do—I quit.

The worker bee stopped working. The pressure was intense, so I wasn't thinking about my professional future when I quit. I was thinking about how I was going to get through the next day. I didn't have this grand plan of how and when I was going to get back into the workforce. I thought my years of work, intelligence, and talent would speak for themselves when I did decide to go back to work. If I decided to go back. How shortsighted that seems now. I never calculated the true cost of stepping back.

Thousands of women who leave the workforce don't have a plan to get back in. There are 3.6 million women on the career sidelines—and we know 93 percent of those who have taken a career break will attempt to return to the workforce. Their children are in school; economically, they *really* need to help support the family again. But many don't even know where to begin, and are afraid that it might be too late.

Is it impossible to get back in? No, but it can certainly feel that way. Is it easy? No, definitely not. Does it require some soul-searching, creativity, and good old-fashioned grit? Yes, yes, yes. The good news is that the workforce is showing positive signs of wanting to bring these women back. But the reality of bringing women back on board or making sure they don't leave in the first place is still quite thorny.

It was an extremely difficult time in my life when I was out of the workforce and trying to figure out what to do. Here's how I turned it around: I just started doing things. I accepted volunteer work where I used skills transferable to the workplace. I networked with anyone and everyone—friends, former business colleagues, people on the soccer sidelines. I took classes. I learned the different social platforms (hello LinkedIn!) and started building my "personal brand." I researched companies. My work skills came back to life much more quickly than I had anticipated. My ambitious self was still there. And when I returned to corporate America, I realized that my career break had actually made me better and more productive in the office—I was more efficient, calmer, positive, and collaborative. All of these skills were honed from being a parent and caregiver.

Honestly, I don't regret quitting. Not for a second. It happened to be the right move for me and my family that I got to know and care for my kids in a different way.

However, I do regret pushing myself to a breaking point and convincing myself that quitting was the only option. I regret not having a transition plan. I regret not knowing the full implications of what quitting would mean for my family and my future earnings. I regret not talking to other women who wrangled with these decisions, too, to get their advice on other possible work options and how to make the road back a little easier. I regret not having anyone helping me figure out what the hell to do. And I'm on a mission to help other women not make my same mistakes.

Meet Stacey

I never thought I would quit my job.

I was walking (running) to the bus one morning when the assistant to my boss's boss called and asked, "Can you take a call from Alan?" She patched me through to Alan Murray, head of digital at the *Wall Street Journal* at the time, who asked if I would be interested in moving from San Francisco to New York to host a new live show on WSJ.com about technology. As a journalist, it was everything I had dreamed of and worked toward for my career—the opportunity to host a live show!

I was ecstatic. I told Alan I was so honored and would love to do it, but needed to talk with my husband, Gabe, first. And then I crashed back to earth. We had just bought a house in San Francisco. And I was pregnant. And not a single soul at my work knew.

That night, my husband, God love him, told me I had to go—that it was everything I had worked for and I needed to seize the moment.

The next day, I picked up the phone to call Alan and told him that, yes, I would love to launch the show in New York, but that I was pregnant (surprise!), so after the show got off the ground, I wanted to come back to San Francisco to have the baby and then run the show from the West Coast. I was nervous, naturally. Would they want me as the host as my belly grew? This was my first pregnancy—I was completely clueless about all of it. Would they think it was best for me to stay in San Francisco given that I was pregnant? Deep down I knew I needed to ask.

"Alan, I promise I'll make it the best show ever . . ."

He said fine. So I moved to New York in January 2010 alone, while my husband stayed in San Francisco to get the house ready for the baby. I planned to go back frequently before my May due date, but my body had other plans. I had placenta previa, a pregnancy condition that can lead to excessive bleeding, and the doctor dissuaded me from too much flying (she suggested taking the train!). So I flew out once and stayed put in New York, got a new team of doctors, and worked and worked and loved every second of the experience, freezing weather and all.

The show was a success. In April, when my San Francisco doctor said it was absolutely time to come home, I cried. I told Alan and everyone who would listen that I would be back in six weeks after having the baby. They all nodded with knowing doubt. We had a generous leave package and I had no clue what my body or mind would go through.

Then came Rory.

Now, it's important to understand that as much as I wanted to host a live television show, I have *always* wanted to be a mother. I can't remember a time when I didn't look forward to having children. So this next life phase was something I yearned for. I just hadn't expected to be having my first baby at age thirty-six—right at the time my career was really flourishing. I hadn't realized how hard it would be to juggle my conflicting desires to be a good mother and stay at the top of my professional game.

I wanted to be in two places at the same time. Thinking about giving up my career felt like killing off part of who I was. My competitive streak knew others would take my role—in my mind they were waiting for me to give it up. Missing my daughter was another kind of death. I needed to be both: a mom and a journalist. The reality of two high-pressure careers and a ridiculous commute for my husband took its toll on me. But I had to figure out how this would work.

At the same time, my peer group was well into having children and I watched friend after incredibly talented and highly educated friend stop working. Their jobs required too much travel and too much face-to-face time. They were missing their kids and didn't have access to flexible work arrangements. All that inflexibility meant that something had to give. These women I admired and respected were dropping out of the workforce because they felt like they had no choice. And I was in the same boat, hoping that someone was going to throw me a life preserver.

I began to do what I was trained to do as a journalist—to look at a problem and start asking questions. I was convinced that there had to be a better way for women—there had to be more flexible employers out there. There had to be resources available to help women through these very predictable work and life transitions. I began searching online for information about companies that supported working mothers and job boards that catered to them.

If employers actually valued women in the workplace, there had to be more respect for these caregiving years. They needed to offer flexibility and real solutions for women pulled between career and child care. It shouldn't be career death to pause or take a break for caregiving. When my second child, Toby, was born, this imperative became all the more clear.

And that's when I took my future into my own hands.

Jen and Stacey Coming Together

We live in a 24/7 work world that's made it impossible to raise children and be "on" all the time. So you're penalized for wanting a nine-to-five life—whether it's through pay cuts or lack of access to promotions or flexible work—to a point that it drives women out of the workforce. And then, to throw salt on the wound, we make it difficult for them to get back into the working world because they've been out doing something important called *raising children*.

This systemic structure is as unfair to women as it is harmful to the economy. Losing female talent and/or not doing the hard work to make senior roles more attractive to women is costing businesses that are desperate for diversity and more women at the top. This is not just about optics; it's about the bottom line. Having more women in mid- and senior-level positions is good for business. Study after study shows that profitability increases when you have a higher percentage of women in leadership roles because you're welcoming analysis and new ideas from a more diverse and well-rounded set of perspectives. When you have the same people from the same backgrounds making the same decisions, truly innovative thinking goes out the window. Women's graduation rates are higher than ever (and more women are graduating from college than men)—we can't afford to lose this brainpower.

And yet, we are.

Since 1962 there had been dramatic growth in the number of women in the workforce in the United States; that number stalled in 2000. We have seen a slight uptick as the economy has strengthened, but compared to foreign counterparts that have seen women pouring into the job market (Germany and France have seen a 20 to 25 percent increase in the same time period), the United States has not. Approximately 26 percent of women of "prime" working age, twenty-five to fifty-four, aren't working, according to the latest data from the International Monetary Fund.

We know that some may see a discussion of staying in or leaving the workforce as one that only a privileged few can have. Does it help to have a spouse (or financially secure parents as we're seeing with millennials) to help cover the costs? Yes. We can't deny that. But we do know that much of the struggle is universal. The IMF and other think tanks argue that a lack of U.S. policies regarding paid leave, affordable child care, and flexible work structures inhibits women's participation in our workforce—policies that affect everyone despite education, income, or marital status.

Women want to work. Pew Research data tells us "the share of mothers saying their ideal situation would be to work full-time increased from 20 percent in 2007 to 32 percent in 2012. And the share saying they would prefer not to work at all fell from 29 percent to 20 percent." It's this data that drove both of us to start companies to stop sidelining women talent.

In early 2013, in San Francisco, Stacey launched Maybrooks, an online career resource for moms. The website was named for her great-grandmother, who went to work during the Great Depression out of necessity and then worked for thirty-five years because she loved it. Stacey wanted Maybrooks to inspire and educate women about career options, and help them find jobs at companies with a focus on family friendliness.

A couple of years later and on the opposite coast, in July 2015, Jen began hatching the idea for Après with Niccole Kroll. Jen never expected to launch a company. But when she couldn't find resources for women like her—women who were at the top of their game and decided to take a career break—she knew she had to help create the solution. Niccole and Jen met through their daughters, who were friends from summer camp, and had both left busy careers (Niccole was a clinical nutritionist and founder of a children's clothing company) to focus on their families.

Jen and Niccole wanted Après to pave the path for women back into the workforce by preparing them and educating companies on why this demographic was a good bet talent-wise for a business.

Just months after launching, a business contact introduced Jen to Stacey. Maybrooks was looking for a partner to scale with and Stacey was impressed with Jen, Niccole, and their team. After one phone call, they hatched a plan. Together, with a bicoastal presence and combined knowledge of the space, they could do more for women together—to stem the flow of women out and pave their way back.

Corporate America's Reaction

Many companies truly want to solve the gender diversity problem but are having a difficult time figuring out a solution. Some are skeptical of women with gaps in their resumes. They want to know that these women will work (they will) and that it is worth their investment in bringing these workers up to speed (it is). And others allow for maternal bias and accept the status quo. Many are fearful of new work structures that would benefit everyone.

There isn't always an earnest desire to fix the widespread push-out of women from the workforce. If there were, there would be more paid leave options (the United States is the only first-world country without a federally mandated benefit), more flexible work opportunities (the structure of how we work has changed very little in the last seventy-five years), more affordable child-care offerings (the biggest expense for working families), better on- and off-ramp opportunities (these are very rare), equal pay, and finally, an end to sexual harassment in the workplace.

It's going to take some real fighting from women and men to swing the door back around. We're seeing this now in the #MeToo and #TimesUp movements—thank goodness. But this is just the beginning of the work to be done. To be honest, it's not rocket science. The pain points on a woman's career path are predictable, and companies need to resource programs to address them.

We need a rallying cry for women and their champions to fight back—and companies need to decide if they are ready to become our allies. It's a tragedy that women should feel undervalued for taking time off to be caregivers and to feel it's overwhelming to get back in. Let's not let one more door slam.

Here's the good news: More organizations like Lyft, Starbucks, and Microsoft are making headlines daily for new and improved parental leave and child-care policies, in some cases demanding more for their contract workers as well as through demands on contractor vendors; New York passed a paid family leave law that covers both child care and elder care. And every day more companies are joining the Après platform, pledging to hire women who have taken a career break and offering paths back through programs like return-to-work internships.

But we're also tired of waiting for *all* of corporate America to follow suit, so we're on a mission to put the tools in women's hands to own their careers.

Carve Your Path

Thanks to our personal experiences as working mothers and the thousands of women we've talked to, we know this to be true: the career path is yours to shape and, whether you know it yet or not, you have the power to create one you want.

If you ride it out and stay in your career or you decide to walk away—if you feel like you have a choice or your bank account tells you otherwise—you are still in the driver's seat, even when it doesn't feel like it. Every decision you make, from where you work to how you work to what you do when you're not working, can help you create the life you want. Will there be obstacles and crappy managers along the way? Yes. It's critical to us that you know you are not alone. We want you to feel the inspiration from the many women around you, charting their own path at the same time.

Here's what else we've learned: the majority of women who have taken career breaks want to work again and, more important, the vast majority of them *have* to work again. Those who take longer breaks often have a big mountain to climb to get back in—be it access (talent application systems, unwilling hiring managers, bias) or confidence. It's only natural: the post-break job search can be overwhelmingly emotional and disheartening. And research shows that after only one year out of the workplace, confidence drops.

Women worry that those years of caring for their kids or volunteering at school won't be appreciated and respected by hiring managers and that their qualifications will be questioned. And though, in reality, there will be some dust on your office-politics, corporate-lingo, and spreadsheet-building skills, the learning curve is not as steep as you imagine. The methods of communication have changed, but the basics of work have not.

We are here to mitigate those fears! To stop perpetuating old concepts that career breaks or part-time work break a career. No career arc is exactly the same, but there are tools that everyone can apply to make the process better—and certainly less messy. Some of the tactics we lay out in this book will help you see the landscape ahead—to think through important decisions, to handle breaks of all shapes and sizes (from a brief maternity leave to a years-long break), and to navigate potential roadblocks before you meet them. Some of the tools will give you the words and smarts/information/ empowering knowledge to talk with employers. Others will give you a framework for decision making that respects and incorporates the personal identity and self-actualization that comes with work, financial realities of a career, and the emotional pull of being a mother.

The questions and emotions that drive women during this stage of life are seemingly endless and the paths, while unique to personal circumstances, are well worn. We know it intimately; we've been through it (and are still in it). We've listened to thousands of women share their own version of the story, many with tears in their eyes, looking for someone to tell them it's going to be okay. And though it can feel like you're alone on the island, like you're the only one grappling with these highly emotional choices, you're not. There are more than 15 million married women working with children under the age of eighteen who find themselves smack in the Messy Middle, when career, caregiving, and parenthood collide (and confusion, challenges, opportunities, and decisions shift into high gear). It's a universal challenge, a midlife career crisis even, that could be considered a cornerstone moment for our generation.

What you'll find here is the stay-at-work, leave-work, return-to-work reality check women actually need. We don't sugarcoat how difficult these decisions can be, but we will help you through them and provide a road map for navigating them so you can make the best decision for you. It's the culmination of the best advice from our Après career coaches and women who have been in your shoes. It's the secrets we've learned from hundreds of companies who are hiring to find out what's really happening—and what women can do if they do take a break to make the transition back to work easier, better, faster, and more beneficial for all.

Whether you're just embarking on the career-plus-motherhood dance, find yourself straddled between caregiving and a job, or dusting the cobwebs off a decision to leave work long ago, we've got you. It's your turn to take back your career path.

Let's get started.

PART I

GETTING AHEAD OF CAREER CONFUSION

CHAPTER 1

WELCOME TO THE MESSY MIDDLE

How will having children affect my career?

The test of life in the Messy Middle is that constant supply of decisions to be made and the seeming weight of *each* decision: Day care versus in-home child care. Part-time versus full-time. Breastfeed versus formula. Organic versus conventional. Taking the promotion versus hitting cruise control. Determinedly plow through versus take a career break.

And while the choices range from big to small, they *should feel* important because they are *new to you*, and it is *your life and your career*. They're also deeply complex thanks to generations of perspectives on what is the "right" choice, information overload from countless websites and op-eds, and a corporate infrastructure rife with bias, be it conscious or unconscious, that often lacks creativity around supporting working mothers.

Juggling career and family is simply overwhelming. And while everyone's circumstances are intrinsically different—no two kids are the same, no jobs, no salaries, no partners, no parents—what women all share is the silent responsibility of making career compromises when others' needs come before ours. The workplace simply doesn't respect the role of caregivers. There's no profit margin on that.

Even if it doesn't feel like it, the truth is, we're all in this together—women and men, those who quit, those who didn't. We, too, underestimated how much having kids would change our career focus. We both felt (and often still feel) that our time at work was often interrupted by home matters, and our focus at home was distracted by finishing work tasks. We have both complained that we weren't being a "good mom" or a "good employee." We have lacked both patience and presence. Our husbands are amazing, but, as is the case for so many women, almost everything related to our home and kids fell to us. And that's just what an ordinary day feels like. Now add to that a situation in which one of your kids really *needs* you. And when that happens it becomes your priority and work takes a definitive backseat, but work doesn't always recognize the outside forces who demand your time. All these factors together can make the decision to leave work all too easy. And the questions can feel endless:

What will happen to my career if I take a break? What kind of mother will I be if I take the promotion I really want? Do I have spit-up on my blazer? Am I wearing matching shoes? How can I negotiate more flexibility? What do I do when my manager discounts me because I'm a mother? Why am I not making as much as that guy? Will my baby remember that someone else took her to the doctor when she was sick? Am I a bad mom because I really love working and don't want to stop?

Our goal here is to take what we've learned and set you up for success—whatever that looks like to you, wherever you find yourself on the career dial: whether you are pregnant and unsure of what to do; sprouting gray hairs from managing life with toddlers, elderly parents, and demanding careers; or getting ready (and a little anxious) to get back to work. To help you make and implement no-regret decisions about your career—and then equip you with the know-how to forge your own path. Whether you decide to leave or stay—no matter what road you take—this is a no-judgment zone. Just as no one can really tell you what being a mother will be like, no one can tell you what your experience will be like trying to have a career and being the parent you want to be.

Getting Clear

Because we all bring different life experiences to the table, work in different fields at different levels, and have our own unique talents, the challenge for you is to get crystal clear on what you want as you approach each transition on the career + motherhood adventure. How you address these decisions *will* shift the course of your life and your career in some way. And while there are no right answers and sometimes you'll be faced with opportunities you never would have dreamed of, you'll want to buckle up for the ride because life can change in an instant no matter what you decide. The babysitter you just hired backs out. The company you work for reorgs your job to another state. You get divorced. People you care about get ill—sometimes very ill. Desires change. A chance conversation while launching a comeback leads to the career of a lifetime.

After spending seven years working with and talking to women at all phases of their careers, we know this: you never know how life will unfold, but you can prepare for the unexpected; being open-minded will in fact open more doors; and no decision is permanent. Having a flexible mind-set will bring you much peace along the way!

Why We Need This Book Now

On paper, we're a much more progressive society.

In 2012, the Pew Research Center found that 79 percent of Americans rejected the concept that women should "return to their traditional role in society." Yet, when it came to experiencing career interruptions, 42 percent of mothers admitted to reducing their work hours to care for a child or family member, whereas only 28 percent of fathers said the same, according to Pew. This is not surprising to us. More than half of Après members surveyed worked for ten to fifteen years before taking a career break. The majority left as managers and directors, just steps from the top, many to allow their partner's career to thrive. These talented and accomplished women worked hard to make work work, and decided to opt out.

As a counterpoint, the LeanIn McKinsey Women in the Workplace 2018 report found that 81 percent of the men *and* women they surveyed say they plan to stay in the workforce, and if they are leaving, it's not to focus on family. However, the Women in the Workplace Report also shows that women enter the workforce at the same pace as men but drop in representation as both men and women climb the career ladder. They found that women are dramatically outnumbered in senior leadership, with only about 1 in 5 C-suite leaders being a woman, and only 1 in 25 being a woman of color.

Here's what this tells us: First, when women do stay in the workforce, gender, race, and "mom" discrimination is preventing them from succeeding. In other cases, we found that some women are conscientiously avoiding the path to the top because they bear witness to the sacrifices—for themselves and their families—it takes to make it. Take Joanie Harrington. Joanie worked in top roles at Barclays for nearly thirty years, and turned down two promotions in the final five years of her career because she didn't want the added responsibility. Joanie is smart, ambitious, and well respected but she's also a realist. She'd paid attention to comments women at the top make about regret, like Indra Nooyi, PepsiCo's first female chief executive, who on her last day of work wrote in a LinkedIn post, "If I'm being honest, there have been moments I wish I'd spent more time with my children and family."

And then there is Beth, who was burned out as a lawyer *before* she even had kids. When she imagined her future self as a parent at her current firm, she saw no vision or a way to make it all work. So when she got a call from her own law school about a position in the career services department, she took the leap. Beth thought it would be good to have a more flexible schedule in place for when she and her husband were ready to start a family. Soon she did get pregnant with her son and went back to work after a twelve-week maternity leave. Everything was fine, Beth says, but as time went on she realized that what she was doing was not intellectually satisfying enough. "I was preparing for the worst-case scenario: having a kid and having no time to focus on my job. I thought I needed a job where I could coast for a few years. I realized that that 'mommy track' job just wasn't enough for me."

So what is driving these highly capable women out of the workforce, having them leave before necessary, or keeping them in middle management roles?

Let us count the ways: It's a job that requires you to fly across the country. It's not having affordable child care . . . or affordable elder care. It's the stacks of unopened mail that create clutter anxiety. It's exhaustion from logging back in after the kids go to bed. It's bosses who don't get it or don't want to get it or assume that you don't want a promotion and more responsibility because you have two kids. It's other parents who don't get it. It's missing networking events for recitals, and missing soccer games for conferences. It's too much email. It's life partners who don't carry their loads at home. No one wants to have it all—we just have too much to do.

Compromises are a fact of life in the Messy Middle, but too often it feels like our hands are completely tied. No matter what you call it—work-life balance, work-life integration, just plain life—women are walking a tightrope. Unless your kids are literally part of your job, there is no integration. There's flexibility. There's remote work. There's the cherished lack of a commute. There are things that make the guilt go away—but it's still there.

The Breaking Point

For most women, the burdens of parenting + career are a bit of a shocker, particularly for college-educated women who are full throttle in their careers and "are surprised by the demands of motherhood," notes the *New York Times* reporter Claire Cain Miller in her article "The Costs of Motherhood Are Rising, and Catching Women Off Guard." Because women are waiting longer to have children—the median age of when women have their first child increased from 26 to 28, in just two years between 2014 and 2016; and the number of U.S. women giving birth between ages 40 to 44 rose to 86 percent, up from 80 percent ten years earlier—and thus have more work experience, many expect that they will be able to continue working, only to find out how stressful today's parenting really is.

More time spent on child care (for both younger *and* older kids—note competition to get into college), women still doing the lion's share of housework, pressure to breastfeed, and so on (whew!) collide head-on with inflexible work structures and 24/7 career demands. Women believe that corporate America will help them make it all happen, will allow for flexibility or less travel, and are let down when they find out that inhospitable work hours are the norm—that many companies, even big ones solving big problems and making lots of money, aren't creative enough to figure this one out. It's disheartening and many either feel stuck or they leave.

As it was for both of us, many women we spoke with see no obvious path for making it doable. Stacey navigated breaking-news live shots with a toddler in the background, while Jen spent countless nights in hotel rooms missing her kids. Traveling as a working parent is tough. Erika in Seattle told us she realized her baby, who came on work trips with her, was traveling more than one of the flight attendants she met. The baby hit premier status before turning one! But it was a more serious incident that put Erika's Messy Middle status into overdrive. "While on a work trip, my day care called and said they would have to call Child Protective Services if my husband or I didn't pick up our five-month-old with pink-eye within thirty minutes," she told us. Her husband, a doctor, was literally attending to a patient having a heart attack and had already said he was unable to meet their time frame. What was she supposed to do? In the end, Erika was too far away to respond and the day care ultimately followed her husband's advice to put the baby in a crib where he wouldn't spread any germs. All was resolved, but not without some racing hearts, stressful phone calls, and a healthy dose of guilt.

In a world of choice, many women are feeling like they have no choice. Or that they have one choice: Is it your career or your kids? The demand of two "big" careers in one household is not to be underestimated, nor is the demand of little children. Without access to large teams of help, it's very difficult to have both partners be full throttle and be caregivers (even Facebook COO and *Lean In* author Sheryl Sandberg admits this now). In 2016 the Center for American Progress found that almost two million parents of kids ages five and younger had to quit a job, turn down a job, or greatly change their job because of issues finding care providers. On the other end of the spectrum, 70 percent of people who help care for aging parents admit to suffering work-related difficulties due to their dual roles, such as cutting back hours or taking a leave of absence. Women feel they're failing at everything, but that's misplaced blame. It's the rigid working structures in corporate America, society's role in equating primary caregiver with mother, and the unbalanced burden of "nonpaid" work that are the real causes of feeling like you can't do it all. When faced with this pressure, one in ten highly educated mothers decide to go.

Inhospitable Working Conditions

On October 26, 2003, Lisa Belkin wrote a controversial *New York Times Magazine* cover story, "The Opt Out Revolution," about a phenomenon where the most educated women in America, hitting their professional stride, were leaving the workforce to stay home with their kids. Belkin profiled eight high-achieving women who had each left the workforce and seemed to happily surrender to full-time motherhood.

"Why don't women run the world?" Belkin wrote. "Maybe it's because they don't want to."

The narrative at that time around opting out became framed in personal choices, with little mention of the societal forces and hostile work environments that pushed many women out of their careers.

As you've likely experienced, there are few child-care benefits. Many companies have made news for offering egg freezing, though just 13 percent of privately employed people have access to paid leave or access to backup child care or stipends to help cover costs. Hourly workers have even less access to options that make work and motherhood feasible. There's no broadly accepted on- and off-ramp.

Despite better technology, there's a lack of access to flexible work options. And when those options do exist, managers aren't trained how to manage and evaluate remote teams and there are often archaic workplace policies that rear their ugly head. Erika worked full-time and remotely for two years after her first baby. After her second child, she wanted to go back part-time. Her boss gave her a choice: part-time or full-time remote. *Not both.* "I went back full-time remote for nine months until the wheels just fell off," she says. We understand companies have to set policies, but most are done with a whole lot of fear and based on assumptions of what works. A more creative approach: test the "both" option.

Moreover, better technology has become a double-edged sword—the phone tethers you to work 24/7 and overwork has become a health hazard leading to burnout. Work continues after leaving the office, after putting kids to bed, into evening hours when laptops fire up again for the notorious second shift. And more than half of Americans don't use all their vacation days. This rhetoric that you have to always be working hard and hustling is damaging to productivity and performance, says Caroline Webb, economist, former McKinsey partner, and author of *How to Have a Good Day.* "There is neuroscience that downtime is just as important as uptime for your brain; when you let your brain rest it can process and connect the information you've been taking in, which can lead to deeper, more valuable thoughts," she says. Employees who do take a break—whether short or long—are more focused and come back with a fresh approach and new motivation.

But there's little incentive or encouragement to take this time out, and many who want to do so fear being penalized.

Inhospitable Living Conditions

Have you ever had a "hospital fantasy"?

In 2013, Katrina Alcorn, a mother of three and a user experience expert and manager, published, *Maxed Out: American Moms on the Brink.* The book chronicles her anxiety, depression, and very personal breakdown, which happened on the way to Target, from parenting and managing a demanding job. Alcorn recovered only to write a powerful manifesto about the toll the 24/7 work environment takes on mothers in particular. In one of her polls she asked participants if they'd ever had a "hospital fantasy," a fantasy that just maybe they would be in a car accident and be injured not too seriously but just enough to warrant a couple of overnights in the hospital where they would be cared for. More than half answered they did.

This doesn't shock us—starting at some point in the 1990s, motherhood became a competition with women vying to be the "best mom" with the "best, most accomplished kids," which usually involves huge time commitments for a million activities. Being a full-time working mom makes it nearly impossible to "win the game" (spoiler: this isn't the game you want to play).

And the lack of equal partnership and unequal division of workload are trying on many women we talked to:

- "I don't think my husband has ever fully grasped the fact that I have two full-time jobs. My 'job' that pays the bills, and being a mother. Forms, doctors' appointments, playdates, sick days, college tours, everything—are all scheduled by me. I have learned to fit them in while I crunch on my salad at my desk, or driving to or from work. He's a great father—just not great at parenthood management."

- "I wish my husband had asked me what I wanted and how I felt. There was just this assumption on his part that I would make the career sacrifice. It took me by surprise because it seemed like we were such partners before."

- "The resentment I felt toward my husband over the fact that he didn't have to factor in breastfeeding as he was making his career decisions was unexpected. For the first time in our eight-year marriage I felt like he had an unfair advantage. It was hard for me to reconcile because I thought of us as equals."

- "Division of workload is always an issue in my house. I shoulder the majority of the housework, the child care, and the household administration. Maybe things would be different if the split was more equal (or felt more equal). A big factor in feeling like I needed more flexibility with work was the looming cloud of everything I'd have to get done in a week."

That list of what you have to get done in a week can be comical: coordinating playdates and car pools, signing up for activities, volunteering, raising good citizens, checking homework, resolving social-emotional conflicts, home repairs, car repairs, vacation planning, bill paying, all while being happy, fun, and loving to everyone around you at all times.

Now backdrop this against career and personal ambition. It's no wonder we feel frazzled.

And yet, despite all of this doom and gloom, for many of us work itself is really satisfying, further complicating the journey. We see this in the gymnastics women do to try to stay in the workforce and the lengths they go to to make it work, to contribute to their families and society.

"As my maternity leave came to a close with my firstborn son, I seriously considered staying home," says Lynn McTeague, a TV producer. "But after much discussion with my husband, I ultimately decided that by continuing in my profession I could offer more to my kids. The comfort of not worrying about money, being able to travel as a family and secure health benefits. And witnessing firsthand that women can be valued in the workplace." That pride you may feel from working is, simply put, priceless.

Looking Ahead

For women who do leave, they may recognize that this decision may impact younger women in the workforce and their own future decisions to opt out. In fact, 17 percent of Après members with less than seven years' work experience, women in their thirties, are saying loud and clear that they fully plan to take career breaks for children and then return to work.

During a time when one would expect to be all in and "killing it," millennials are quitting their jobs at a dramatic pace (43 percent expect to leave their job within two years). These late-twenty-somethings without kids are leaving in search of a job with a better workplace culture and access to flexibility (a perk not just revered by parents). "Yes, I plan to keep working after I have children, but I am already struggling keeping up and balancing my career, relationships, social life, and health," said Tasmia, a thirty-year-old HR professional from Chicago. "I cannot imagine how I will be able to still manage all this plus be a mommy and give my best work." Or they're burned out and leaving the rat race entirely to take a break "while they still can."

These young women have been watching the story unfold

ahead of them—being inspired by women who make it work, and witnessing others who struggle. They view a career break as a reset; a moment to gain perspective; a chance to take advantage of the world's possibilities without dependents. They're not lazy and entitled, as so many mislabel this generation. They feel that by doing this they will be on the right road and more prepared for when the time comes to balance career and kids.

What all these women share, from Generation X to Z, is the voice in their head asking, Is this my path? What makes me happy, what matters most? And, what should I do about it?

The Many Paths of Career + Motherhood

Stacey was rising through the ranks until she decided a part-time schedule was what she needed; Jen was a workaholic who never thought she would quit. But sometimes taking a break leads to a complete career pivot or new passion that yields a business. That's what happened to both of us, who each started her own business to help others in the Messy Middle. We're in good company, too: women are starting businesses at a rapid clip, nearly 1,800 per day, Amex Open Forum estimates.

For many, there is no choice to not work. Middle-class life is now 30 percent more expensive than twenty years ago and most feel like they're on shaky economic ground, says Alissa Quart, author of *Squeezed: Why Our Families Can't Afford America.*

For others, taking a career break is a privileged decision. They have a supportive partner who can earn enough to sustain their family and loss of wages for a few years or they have carefully saved for this time. They are seizing this coveted opportunity to raise children. As Stacy Brown, founder of restaurant chain

Chicken Salad Chick, told Guy Raz in his podcast, *How I Built This*, "I always knew I would start a business. But I also knew I couldn't do it all at once. Now was my time to be a mother."

And for more, working is in their DNA. In 2013, 37 percent of working mothers said their ideal situation would be to work full-time, up from 21 percent of working mothers in 2007. Women said they "felt like themselves" at work and didn't want to quash their ambition, or said that "work helps me be a better mom because I appreciate my kids so much more when I'm away from them." We get it, we feel it, too!

It's the Long Game

Here's the good news: the Messy Middle is temporary. It's a short five-ish years before kids are in kindergarten, when the infrastructure of school starts to normalize the chaos of the toddler years. Realizing this is a finite period of your life is key to keeping your cool when navigating the heavy-feeling decisions along the career-plus-motherhood highway. Hats off to Anne-Marie Slaughter, who says it well—your career is a long game. Slaughter's 2013 essay in the *Atlantic*, "Why Women Still Can't Have It All," kicked off a national debate as she publicly recounted her struggle to manage her career and teenagers while a senior advisor to Hillary Clinton in the State Department.

As Slaughter told an audience at SXSW in 2013, when you're in the thick of it—babies, sick parents, work pressures, looming promotions—it can feel like the world is closing in on you and you have no choice. But, she said, women who want a family and a fast-track career can have both, with help. Help of family, friends, day care. Sometimes one may take a back burner to the other. Maybe that means taking your career off the fast track for a few years. If the average age of women having children is twenty-eight, and the average age of retirement is sixty-six, that means we have about forty years to play with in there.

Forty years! Just saying it out loud should bring some perspective.

HOW COMPANIES CAN SHINE:
Take stock of your practices and policies.

Workplace culture is one of the biggest factors in a woman's decision to stay or leave a company and/or the workforce. So what matters? The strength of a company's policies, good managers who have the training and tools to execute those policies, and the understanding that employees won't get penalized for taking advantage of those policies. Here's what companies can do:

1. **Review your company's benefits and policies.** What are the current benefits and are they working? Does your company offer paid leave? For how long? Is it inclusive of all parents— women, men, adoptive parents? Does your company offer child-care benefits? The more time and support a woman has postdelivery, the more likely she is to return to work. What are the flexible work policies? Does the company's technology enable remote work? When workers feel more ownership of their time, they're more focused and productive and feel more positive toward their employer. Has the company made the appropriate changes to these policies in the wake of the #MeToo movement? Take a cue from Google and abandon forced arbitration policies in employee contracts. What about salary transparency to ensure there is no gender salary gap? Is there a clear communication path for reporting

harassment or discriminatory behavior and do your employees know about it? Your answers to these questions signal that you value an equal, fair, respectful, and inclusive culture.

2. **Create a benefits and policies task force.** Gather a diverse group of employees from various departments to understand how you can improve your culture, inclusion, and benefits. Survey your employees anonymously. What do they need to be successful at work? What are women telling you? How many women have come to Human Resources asking for a creative strategy to stay in the game—how many have been heard and how many have been denied? Be sure to probe into your culture, too—do employees feel comfortable saying when they're uncomfortable? Be transparent in your findings—let employees know these are things the company is thinking and caring about. Make a wish list of future benefits and start tackling it. That's the ultimate goal.

3. **Review your diversity statistics.** How many women work at the company? How many work in leadership roles? How many minorities are represented? How do you measure up to other companies? If you don't already have a Diversity and Inclusion initiative or group, create one. If you do, empower it.

CHAPTER 2

THE BIG DECISION

Should I Stay or Should I Go?

Should I take a career break?

It's a pivotal question that leads to a deeper look into the practical *and* emotional parts of your life. There are financial implications, for sure, but the answer will likely also change how you see yourself. It may open doors you never knew existed and conjure up unexpected emotions. It's an exploratory time: You'll think about how you were raised and the decisions your parents made. You'll look to your friends, peers, moms at the playground, moms keynoting a women's conference and ask yourself, is that the life I want? Does that align with my values?

It's a question that's just as difficult to tackle as "Where do you see yourself in five years?" No one can predict where they will be in five years, just like the fact that it's nearly impossible to prepare for what your career will look like once you have kids. Or when you have a sick kid. Or a sick parent. Life changes, perspectives change. Jen never thought she would

quit. She *loved* working. But she did. As do 10 percent of educated women.

It's a choice that cycles on repeat throughout your career,
even if you never imagined you would consider it. It's a decision
that evolves and grows. One you think you have the answer to,
and then something happens and you choose to go another way.
And that's okay—our goal is to help you feel secure in your choice
for this moment right now.

Because most women hold themselves to such high standards
of perfection—that we *can* do it all, or at least *try* to do it all—
the thought of leaving the workforce is scary. But never make a
career decision out of fear—or the pursuit of perfection. Instead,
arm yourself with knowledge and confidence to understand the
nuances of what you're potentially losing and gaining. Some
losses are obvious (money) and others you might not expect (work
friends). Some gains might be totally unexpected (deciding to
pursue an entirely new career).

Career breaks come in all shapes and sizes—there's the
maternity leave "break," the get-me-through-the-newborn-phase
break, the no-kids-I'm-just-burned-out break, I'm-going-to-wait-
until-my-kids-are-in-school-break, and the eek-how-long-has-it-
been (?!) break.

Sharpen your pencils because we're going to help you outline
your options and hit you with the ins and outs, the good and bad,
the silver linings and the emotional roller coasters. You will need
to dig deep to know yourself and decide what's best for you. This
is a personal decision, but we've heard the same questions and
concerns over and over again and know the universal challenges.
Based on our research, these are the top ten things to consider, or
the ultimate should-I-take-a-career-break quiz, as you face this
career choice.

Top 10 Things to Consider

Number 1: Money
Can you afford to leave your job?

Career and money are so tightly wound together, it's no surprise that this decision starts with its financial impact on your present and your future. Can you afford to make a job change right now? How will your family cover its monthly expenses without your salary? While it's true that numbers never lie, there are hidden costs and compromises to consider when doing the math.

First, focus on your day-to-day finances. Take the time to log all your monthly expenses on a spreadsheet and categorize them into columns: Musts, Wants, Work, No Work. Yes, it seems like a chore—very few people enjoy making a budget, and in fact only 41 percent of Americans say they have a budget. But in this case, you can't pass Go without one.

In the Musts column, list your core bills and expenses (housing, utilities, car, insurance, food, and so on). For the Wants column, be honest with your spending habits and think about what's important to you as a person and a parent to thrive and not just survive. This may include opportunities for dance classes, sports, dinners out, and family vacations (even inexpensive ones). Be realistic about yourself, too: If you really hate cooking, factor in the cost of takeout. If you love TV, put your cable and streaming costs there, too.

For the Work column, note your expenses related to your career: commuting, dry cleaning bills, work clothes, pricey lunches. This will be your bonus! For the last No Work column, think about what benefits you're receiving as an employee. Do you get any corporate discounts on your bills—if so, what's the full rate? Add in the difference in this column. Do you get a company cell phone or do they pay for your wireless bill? Do you have to give back your laptop? Will you need to buy a new one? What about digital subscriptions, museum passes, or other random perks?

Then there is health care. Does your family use your company-provided health benefits? If so, research the cost of your other options like your partner's coverage plans or privately purchased plans. Dental and vision can be expensive out of pocket, too (cleanings cost an average of $150: multiply that by two times a year and how many family members need to go). Also, if you need to switch providers, compare what's covered. If you have a preexisting condition or a standing date with your acupuncturist, you want to make sure you're not going to be hit with a huge out-of-pocket expense.

Look at the math. Is it possible to cover it all without your salary?

This probably feels overwhelming; we know. Throwing numbers at the sheet will not only help you see if making a big career change is a possibility, but creating a budget will also help you decide just how much change to your lifestyle it will take to work out financially.

This is when the compromises come in: Based on this new budget, which expenses can you live without? Which are non-negotiable? Would you have to move? Where can you get creative? Can you cut the cord and subscribe to Netflix and Hulu only? Don't rule out the possibility that if you start saving aggressively *now* you can build a fund in a year or two to support your decision to leave.

If you're fortunate to have a partner with a significant income, this exercise might seem unnecessary and tedious; that your salary goes straight to savings, so it won't impact your day-to-day living. You probably even skipped most of this section. But we caution you to not glance over number 2, the financial loss most people ignore.

Number 2: Future Financial Losses
What will quitting cost you in the future?

We often hear women approach the question with simple back-of-the-napkin math: *My salary won't cover the cost of a babysitter, so I had no choice!* And while there's no question child care is a huge expense (it's the next factor we dig into), it's not as clear-cut as it may seem. The gut reaction is to say it's not worth it to keep working. We get it. The net-net doesn't always look good and makes it an "easy" decision.

But the lifetime cost of taking a five-year break is significant.

The Center for American Progress, a Washington, D.C.–based think tank, created a career break cost calculator that requires one to rethink the formula **length of break** × **salary = cost of career break.** The calculator combines lost income, lost income growth, and lost retirement benefits. A sample calculation for a twenty-six-year-old woman taking a five-year career break results in a $467,000 financial loss. A substantial portion of this figure is lost retirement benefits and the accrued interest lost over her lifetime.

These figures provide a compelling counterargument to the often-cited notion that women should take a career break because child care is expensive. We want you to be aware of this perspective and the financial implications that will follow you before you make a decision.

Look at your financial savings plan: If you have a 401(k) plan with your company, research what will happen to it (can you roll it over to another brokerage penalty-free?). How much will you lose on matched contributions? Will you still be able to contribute to a retirement fund or college savings plan while you're out of the workforce? Is this okay for your family?

Money equals security. If you were to quit, and life delivered lemons (your partner loses his or her job, your furnace goes kaput and you need to replace it), would you be okay for a period of time? We know, every family's financial situation is different. Some may be savers, and have the emergency fund to show for it; some may have security blankets in the form of generous family members; and others may be in a partnership with someone who is making enough money to cover it all.

Number 3: Child Care
Who is going to take care of the kids?

The impact of the rising cost of child care is being felt throughout the United States, where the birth rate just dropped to the lowest since 1987. We have a theory: student debt is overwhelming, housing prices are rising, and there has been a steady increase in the cost of living since 1998.

But this isn't just exclusive to the United States. Portugal and Singapore have seen a steady decline in birth rates, too. China, for example, recently lifted its one child per family ban, but the predicted baby boom just hasn't happened—Chinese residents are still having only one kid. One country on the rise: Sweden, which is known for its generous family policies, like a sixteen-month parental leave. Coincidence? We think not.

Child care is the mega-expense that tends to make or break your decision. It can *keep you in* the workforce when you're earning a good salary or are the breadwinner (42 percent of all working women). One woman told us, "Before my son arrived I planned to go part-time, then I realized how much child care costs would impact our cash flow and decided to work full-time and get a higher-paying job." It's one of the biggest financial strains on a family. Nearly a third (31 percent) of parents say that child-care costs have caused major stress, according to a poll from NPR, the Robert Wood Johnson Foundation, and the Harvard Chan School of Public Health. Of those, 71 percent say that these costs have represented a "very serious" or "somewhat serious" financial problem.

It can also *keep you out* of the workforce, even if you didn't want to go. Liz Tracy, a writer, didn't want to quit working, but she and her partner simply couldn't afford child care. She was working as a full-time museum grant writer at Pérez Art Museum in Miami when she found out she was pregnant. They decided to move to Boston because her partner needed health insurance for a chronic condition and under Massachusetts's progressive health care system he could get insured right away. But she couldn't keep her job. Her partner had a steady job as assistant manager at a UPS Store, but his salary would have been just enough to cover day-care costs. So Liz started to freelance at night when her baby was sleeping (no easy feat). What Liz didn't know at the time was that Boston also offers subsidized day care. Once a family member clued her into it, this was the help she needed. "I knew about Head Start for preschool kids, but I didn't know there were programs that helped working people with financial support for day care," says Liz. They had to do mounds of paperwork and wait a full year for their son to be accepted, but she says it was worth it to have an affordable child-care solution that allows her to get back to work. Now they're moving to Washington, D.C., to be closer to her parents and because D.C. also offers free pre-K for three-year-olds. Side note: New York has started this, too, with its Universal Pre-K program—check the National Women's Law Center's site for state-by-state guidelines.

Child care can also be taxing on your emotions. Searching for the perfect program or person (and managing this new relationship!) is stressful; there's no question about that. If you don't have family around who are willing to pitch in, you will need to trust your child with a professional center (day care) or babysitter (or nanny or au pair). For many of the women we've talked to, no amount of background checks, reference calls, or drop-in visits could eradicate the nervousness about this process. If this sounds like you, know that it gets easier and your anxiety will wane as your comfort level grows.

The bigger struggle is learning to let go of the guilt. Even when you have a caregiver with the biggest heart who has become a part of your family, there can be a twinge of envy that you're not the one pushing baby on the swing or washing away the tears after a fall. Yearning for those moments of comfort when you're sleep deprived and a newborn's needs seem all-encompassing can make it feel like there's no other choice but to quit. Just remember, nothing is permanent. Patience is key. It is possible to find quality care.

Number 4: Your Relationship
How will this affect your partnership?

Many of the women we spoke with said their partners were completely supportive of their final decision to stay or go. Whether it was a "don't worry we will figure it out" mantra or "I will support you however you choose to make this all work," their partners were there for them. They said all the right things.

But for some, this felt like the partner was offloading the decision onto mom. "Whatever you want" sounds great, but in reality it is a lot of pressure. It becomes *your* decision versus *our* decision, and one that is positioned (even if well intentioned) as yours to do "whatever will make you happy" versus "this is good for our family," and could easily backfire in the future. Will your partner resent you when you aren't earning money?

When Gabe and I discussed me going part-time and then quitting to start my own business, we talked some about the financials but largely about what it meant for our family, Stacey says. It put more burden on him financially, but the flexibility for me fulfilled a dual desire to have one of us more available to our kids. During one year when Toby was diagnosed with asthma and we were at the doctor regularly, Gabe revealed what a relief it was that I could be with Toby and take care of him, and that this allowed him to work without the stress of worry.

Many times the partner's life does become a lot less stressful when a mother decides to give up her career. When a woman is home full time, almost all of the day-to-day parenting issues are taken care of. Yet it's not as simple as that. There is a shift in power dynamics that happens when one person's work life changes. Even when you have the most supportive of spouses, it is inevitable that you will feel a sea change in the relationship when you no longer contribute to the family finances and you do not have your own paycheck.

It's really important to stop and consider what a career break means for you *personally*. One woman told us she wished her partner made her stop and really think about leaving and what her life would look like. They talked through the logistics, but not the emotions involved: What does it mean for finances beyond daily expenses (do you now get an, eh, allowance?). Is there going to be more expected on you to manage the household in addition to the child care (most likely yes) and are you going to be resentful of that (most likely yes)?

Ask yourself: Does one of you hold on to traditional notions of what a "good mom" or a "good wife" does? Your immediate response is probably, no, of course not. But the reality is when one partner is home, there is an expectation that they do more of the "house-work" because, you know, "they're not working." And taking care of children all day is a breeze (ha!), which gives you tons of time to make dinner, do all the laundry, clean the house, get the car washed, call the plumber. . . .

During the first couple of years of my career break, I didn't notice this as much because I was focused on raising my small children, Jen says. But as time marched on, I became more and more frustrated with feeling detached from the family finances and not having my own paycheck. This was entirely self-imposed but I used to be a major financial contributor and now I felt like I needed to talk with David before buying a nice pair of shoes! It wasn't like I had an allowance, but I felt like I lost a little financial freedom and would feel guilty when I did spend money on myself. That got old, fast.

You need to talk about clear expectations for yourselves and each other before you make this decision. After quitting, many women confessed that they experienced an unexpected free fall into old-school gender roles, with "the man going to work" and the "woman taking care of the kids." Margaret, a researcher for a public policy think tank, said, "He hopped on the stay-at-home-mommy train realllllly quickly. He had visions of me holding his pipe and slippers." And although there might be more financial constraints, it is easier for the family when one person stays home. There are fewer scheduling conflicts, fewer Saturdays spent running errands. Your story can be different, if you both communicate what you want and need ahead of time.

Number 5: Your Support System
Who can help you?

When you're deciding to make a career change, look around: Do you have a wide circle to support you on your new path? Do you have family around to pitch in with child care when the babysitter inevitably calls in sick? One woman told us, "As a single mom, the decision was mine, but I wanted to get my family's buy-in, too. My extended family supported the change because they knew I was unhappy long before I admitted it to them." There's a perception that modern families are spread apart, but about 51 million, or one in six Americans, live in households with at least two adult generations—roughly 23 percent of blacks, 22 percent of Hispanics, and 13 percent of whites. The average adult lives only eighteen miles from his or her mother.

Now, it isn't clear who is taking care of whom in this scenario—this research shows that in many instances couples are moving to be closer to aging parents. When women are having babies later, the idea that parents are going to be able to help out is decreasing as they get older.

In Boston, writer Liz Tracy found herself in a new city where they had no family or friends. She underestimated the importance of having someone to call up and help out with the baby when she needed last-minute help or just a break; someone you can vent to, or someone who can meet you in the park for adult conversation. New mom friendships happen, but they take time to build. Do you have allies who are around during the day? Whether to help you get through the hours (if you choose to quit) or to pick up your kid in a pinch (if you choose to work), these women (and men) are key to your survival.

Number 6: Workplace Culture
Are you at a good company for working parents?

Where you work—especially the culture, attitude, and support toward working mothers—is another huge factor in a woman's decision to stay or leave the workforce. How the combination of a company's policies and unspoken expectations (for example, does anyone actually use the company's flexibility program?) will dictate the score of how parent friendly a workplace is. Norms around paid leave, vacation time, salary transparency, and work hours can clue you in to how supportive a company is of all its employees. That's the top-down approach to culture. But how employees feel and act toward one another also drives culture. Do you feel the need to hide your family life? Is there an unstated but widely held company view that family obligations take you off track? Are there implicit face-time politics? Do you feel undermined by management? Is there a spirit of collaboration or competition? It's a gut check.

After meeting with leaders at hundreds of companies, from law firms and financial institutions to start-ups and nonprofits, we can tell almost instantaneously if the office has a family-friendly vibe. Employees are happy to be there, there is leadership buy-in, and it's obvious everyone believes in their company values—it's not all talk. Employees have autonomy over their schedule and are free to make decisions about their time, whether that's as big as taking vacation time or something as small as feeling empowered to take a personal day.

Assessing if a company is family friendly/female friendly will be an essential tool throughout your career as you make decisions about where to work. But how do you do this? Many companies don't make concrete data about paid leave, family-friendly policies, and general working parent happiness easy to obtain. LinkedIn profiles don't mention it. *Working Mother* magazine's Best 100 list tracks representation, parental leave, family support, and flexibility, but it's refreshed just once a year. Sites like Work180, Glassdoor (to a degree), and Great Places to Work are working hard to make cultural cues more transparent through largely crowd (women employee)–sourced data. Tech has been the leader in releasing data around percentage of women in the workplace as a force function for improving gender and diversity representation. In fact, California passed a new law that requires publicly traded companies headquartered in California to have at least one woman on their boards of directors.

Look to see if the company publishes information about how many women work there and at what level, if they're forthcoming about their flex time and paid leave policies. What are they saying to the media about company culture? Those are strong clues to the work environment, but sadly, what companies are saying publicly doesn't always tell the whole picture. Women spoke of widespread sexism at start-ups in Liza Mundy's *Atlantic* article, "Why Is Silicon Valley So Awful to Women?" These anecdotes were confirmed by a report from the Center for Talent Innovation that found that women leave their jobs in tech at a 45 percent higher rate than men. And the reason is not always family (only 27 percent cited that). Instead, for these women, the report stated, it's the "workplace conditions, a lack of access to key creative roles, and a sense of feeling stalled in one's career." Plain and simple, it's bias.

Key takeaway: As you map out your career, it's good to take a close look at where you work now or where you want to work. If you love your job but hate the culture, it's likely not going to work. If you love the culture, you'll likely find a way to make the job work. So why not start with culture first?

Number 7: Access to Flexibility
Could you ask for an alternate schedule?

For many working parents, flexibility—of schedule, total hours, work location—is the solution they crave to be able to feel happier at work and at home. Research from the IBM Smarter Workforce Institute found having flexible working arrangements led to "higher feelings of balance and job satisfaction." It's also the number one search criteria for women looking for a new role, according to a study by PricewaterhouseCoopers, and the main reason that millennials leave jobs without it.

"There are many times when the balance feels off, when there is too much going on at home and I'm missing things that seem important to my kids," says Emily Hill, a mom of three and CFO. "But I feel very lucky to have found a rewarding career both intellectually and financially that affords me a fair bit of flexibility."

Countless women we talk to cite lack of creativity in schedules, long commutes, and untenable travel among the reasons they leave. Research also has shown that of the 30 percent of women who drop out of the workforce after having a child, 70 percent would have stayed if they had access to flexibility.

What's the situation where you work? Do you have flexible options? Flexibility can mean a million different things. For some women, it's a feeling—an uncodified agreement or a mutual trust, that it's okay to leave at five to get home for dinner or to work from home on parent–teacher conference day. Maybe you leave early every Thursday to go to basketball practice. For others, whether it's job share, part-time, work-your-own hours, or remote work, it's a contract that's in place where everyone—your team, managers, and colleagues—is cognizant of your flexible schedule. And, if there are flexible options, do people take them?

Cutting back on your hours instead of quitting is a path many working moms take. Employed mothers are nearly five times more likely to work part-time than fathers. And while working a reduced schedule or remotely comes with its own challenges, asking for any or all of the above is worth it if you're considering giving notice anyway.

Number 8: Your Identity and Goals
What does success mean to you? What do you value?

It can be downright scary to just stop working, whether you've been doing it for five or fifteen years. Here's what women told us frightened them the most about making the transition.

- Not being taken seriously.
- Losing your identity.
- Not helping others solve complex problems.
- Being bored.
- Watching colleagues (and your assistant) pass you by.
- Being out of your element as a stay-at-home mom.
- Not having others value your opinion.
- Giving up the career you've worked toward your whole life.

There's no question the transition can be rough, but that shouldn't be the guiding factor here. First, think about your ideal day-to-day life: What do you think will bring you the most joy? For some women, identity and career is a package deal. It's how they define themselves and success. For them, holding on to a part of their career is what makes them thrive and be a better mom. For other women, being able to be home with their children is the ultimate success story. And doing that feels like a win. Some people can't handle staying home all day—some people love it.

Everyone is different—there is no "perfect mom" or "perfect career woman."

Take your cue from Benjamin Franklin and write out a good old-fashioned pro/con list. Don't fill it out as though your mother or best friend will look at it. Fill it out with what *you* value. Don't let what society deems a good mom/good employee/good wife dictate your list. You may feel pressure, whether societal, familial, or internal, to stay home because it's "what a mother is supposed to do," but considering staying home as a necessary sacrifice only perpetuates the image of mother as martyr. Make the decision based on what you value—not what others tell you to value. Maybe that means missing soccer games or the ukulele sing-along. Moms *are* held to a higher standard and that can easily be internalized if you don't hold on to your identity. Give this some major consideration. Think about what makes you tick.

Everything you think you might lose by leaving you'll balance out with how much you gain: irreplaceable time with your kids, a fresh perspective on life, time to discover who you might be, and the chance for reinvention. Know that you can take a career break and still be ambitious. It just looks a bit different. If your goal is to be a managing director, a career break will slow that path. But you might take a career break and think, why did I ever want to be an MD in the first place? And that realization could open new doors.

"If you're not working more than full-time and bucking for the C-suite, that doesn't mean you're not ambitious," says Kathryn Sollmann, author of *Ambition Redefined*. "You can be an ambitious part-time worker. You can be an ambitious admin assistant." You can be an ambitious person while being on a career break by continuing to learn, grow, and evolve. And your choice doesn't have to be permanent—you can go back to work.

Number 9: Your Job
Do you want to return to what you're doing?

A career break will change your career. A decade after Belkin's "Opt Out Revolution," Judith Warner revisited those women who left their careers in 2003, in her own *New York Times* piece, "The Opt-Out Generation Wants Back In." What Warner found was that some of the women who ten years earlier felt empowered to drop out were now regretting their choices. One who gave up her high-paying job at Oracle to stay home in her big house to care for her three kids was now divorced, living in a rental apartment across from a supermarket, and making 20 percent of her former salary. Many of these women had believed that their degrees were their insurance policies and when they were ready—if they wanted to—they could jump back into the workforce and pick up where they left off.

The reality, we now know, is much grimmer. Studies show that nearly 90 percent of women who take time off from paid work will reenter the workforce but only 40 percent will find the full-time, satisfying work they want. And two-thirds of women who take a career break return to lower-skilled roles with an average salary cut between 12 and 32 percent.

Scary stats, yes, but a career break doesn't have to kill your career. Those figures don't take into account positive changes happening: more women creating new options for themselves, starting businesses, and a renewed corporate awareness of (though not necessarily action toward) the challenges for working parents. When you take a bad situation and make it your own, you change the narrative.

If you were to quit, how easy would it be to return to work? In many industries, like finance and advertising, once you take your foot off the gas pedal, it can be hard to return to the same level. Look around. Are there older moms who took time off? Where are they now? Are you okay with coming back at a lower level than where you are now?

Some industries are a bit more forgiving with career breaks. Education and law, for instance, offer a bit more freedom for people to come on and off the ramp as long as they do so in the parameters of the industry. In most states, teachers, for instance, can apply for unpaid contractual child-care leave and are guaranteed a job placement for up to four years after the birth of a child.

Are you open to the possibility of change to a different field after a break? For some this might be a great way to reinvent themselves into an area of more passion than the career they took right out of college. For some it becomes a time to focus on something very meaningful, such as work at a mission-driven company or nonprofit. For others it's a strategic decision based on the type of work required. One woman decided to pivot from her marketing role to writing because she could do that job from anywhere.

What about your skills? Could you freelance or consult while on a break? Our best piece of advice is to always keep one foot in the door and use your skills in some capacity. Creative and technical fields tend to sync up with the gig economy quite well, but there are more admin and management roles that do the same. From bookkeeping to event management, having transferable skills will make taking a break easier.

Number 10: Timing
Do I have to decide right now?

It's when you're fruitlessly trying to find a quiet place to pump or after back-to-back work trips that the answer is a resounding yes, that something needs to change right this second. But before you invest your energy into trying to make a decision, can it wait six months?

You don't want to make a hasty decision—especially during big life transitions, whether your hormones are still evening out three months after the baby is born or you missed the first day of kindergarten, or during particularly challenging workdays. Patience is key in these moments. We recommend going back to work for a while post-baby just to see how it goes before deciding your path.

Making a decision based on assumptions (I will miss his first steps; he won't bond with me) is a huge energy drain. Jen recently asked her eight-year-old if he remembered his big fifth birthday bash and he didn't! We're not saying to stop analyzing your options. You need to go into every decision with your eyes wide open, but just take some time to check in and ask yourself: Do I need to decide this now or is there a good reason to wait?

Delay Decision Making

What if you kept going until your child was ten? That's a trend we see particularly with women in finance. They push through the early years to reach a career milestone (or earn a large package) and then "retire early" just as their kids are hitting the emotionally challenging tween stage. The truth is, while babies are needy, teens are demanding in a whole different way. When Joanie Harrington's children were eleven and nine, they made the case to their mom: we need you home. They articulately listed the reasons why. Babies can't do that. Joanie agreed and embarked on an eighteen-month transition-me-out plan with Barclays. She has never been happier. She is volunteering more and is finding time to do things she put off for years.

Making a major career change should be carefully considered, and if you resign rashly, you may make a decision you'll later regret. Give yourself time to explore the problem and the potential solutions, because there are many solutions! You'll know what's right for you and your family.

When You Can't Decide What to Do

Making this decision is one of the hardest parts about life in the Messy Middle. If you're still unsure, ask yourself these three questions:

1. **What is the most challenging part of my current situation?**

    Quitting can seem like a quick fix. Ask yourself, what's the hardest thing you're dealing with right now that is making you question your career choices? Which part is stressing you out? Is it job related or home related? Is there a way to mitigate or resolve the stress? Can someone help you with this?

    In figuring out whether to stay or go, it's useful to unpack the difference between the perceived reality of what a job change might look like and the reality of actually making that change. Try to imagine what it would feel like sitting at a new desk, in a new job, with new colleagues. Then, imagine what it would be like to stay at home.

    Be secure in the knowledge that your current status is temporary. This might be a bumpy phase in a long life.

2. **What scares me most about the decision?**

    What actions could I take to make sure I have all the information I need to actually make this decision? How could I get out of my own head and take action or experience something that would help me get a sense for how this new thing might feel?

    We are all afraid; you are not alone. Talk about it. If you

don't have a community at work find some online or in your neighborhood. Share your truth. Lift each other up.

3. **What do I really want?**

Eleanor Roosevelt famously said, "Do what you feel in your heart to be right—for you'll be criticized anyway." You're most likely not thinking about this decision in a vacuum. You're going to talk to a million people to get their opinions and hear their stories. Don't make this decision because of outside voices. Or subtle judgment being passed along. Maybe you've been shamed by other moms for not knowing a swim teacher's name, or not knowing that a kid has a nut allergy. Maybe your mom doesn't like you working; maybe your partner has dropped hints that it would be nice for someone (ahem, you) to help out with the family finances.

Take it easy on yourself. Trust your gut.

Yes, money, child care, and everything else we outlined are complex considerations that can impact the health and happiness of your family. But at the end of the day, ask yourself: What do you want right now? What do you want in the future? Putting the needs of others ahead of yours is probably familiar, but consider that making decisions about your career that you don't feel in your heart are right may sow the seeds of resentment.

HOW COMPANIES CAN SHINE:
Offer (generous) paid leave.

It's extremely costly to companies when women leave and new people need to be recruited and trained—KPMG estimates this cost to businesses to be $47 billion globally each year. Companies that are offering generous paid leave will keep women talent from leaving and also subtly state, "We don't penalize mothers." Google says the number of new mothers who quit after having a baby decreased by 50 percent after it increased its paid leave from twelve weeks to eighteen. And paid leave for fathers destigmatizes caregivers as women only. Eighty-six percent of women are mothers by the time they're forty-four, so if your company is truly committed to gender diversity, it is incredibly important to be supportive during this time. Here's what companies can do:

1. **Compare your company's paid leave policy to highly rated employers.** All twenty of the largest companies now offer paid leave and the Society for Human Resource Management finds the number of companies offering paid leave is one in three, up from one in six since 2010. Analyze what your company can afford to do, and have policies for those who adopt, who use surrogates, and for paternity leave, and partners, too. Use a gender neutral approach to the term *primary caregiver*.

2. **Create a culture that encourages taking paid leave.** Ensure that women and men take advantage of paid-leave policies—and not feel stressed that they have to return to work earlier than expected. Enforce your paternity leave: it's great for fathers, but helps mothers during recovery time, too. Companies in return will have the benefit of a more productive workforce. No one does their best work when they're sleep deprived.

3. **Communicate your policies and open the dialogue before and after the leave.** Have programs for new parents before they take leave. One woman told us, "I wish that my employer would've

offered a session for anticipating parents (men and women) where they walked us through the benefits that they provided for parents. It could have covered parental leave, emergency child care, and even milk transport." Then offer programs that help new parents transition back to work. Consider postleave transitions back such as a part-time or reduced schedule. The law firm Orrick (which provides twenty-two paid weeks and job protection for nine months) allows for a 50 percent workload "expectation" during the first month back. Offering paid leave at all is a major step toward re-taining talent, but go a step further—don't let her quit. Say, "What would help you stay?" Then act on those policies.

CHAPTER 3

THE CASE FOR STAYING

Am I all in?

Spreadsheets? Check. Calendar planning? Check, double check. Maximized commute time and no water cooler chitchat? Check, check, check. Backups for backups? Naturally.

We know you know her. She's a working mom and she is owning it. They're some of the most efficient, productive people we know. We dare you to find a working mom who isn't laser focused on her priorities. She knows there's a bull's-eye on her back so she'll work harder, faster, and better to prove others wrong.

If this sounds like you, be confident in this because being a parent will actually make you better at what you do.

The decision to forge ahead in your career is a big decision, a good one for many people, and also a reality for many people. The majority of women return to work after their first baby. And we know plenty of women who never quite committed to their maternity leave, doing deals on the phone while bouncing and feeding, or bringing baby to a conference. We talked to countless women who happily continue to work and whose families continue to thrive on many levels. No matter your situation, you can do it, too.

The key to surviving the Messy Middle of your career is to figure out what works best for you. Is it working full time? If yes, then do everything in your power to ensure you and your family are set up for success.

When Amy Henderson, cofounder and CEO of Tendlab, had her third child she was anxious about how it would impact her career. "I decided to reach out to other mothers I admired to learn from them if it were possible to both show up for parenting and build a successful career," Henderson shared on LinkedIn. "In between round-the-clock feedings and diaper changes, I paced the house with my sleeping infant in my arms, my neck kinked to hold the phone between my cheek and shoulder while I whispered into the receiver: How are you doing it? What I unearthed in these conversations shocked me. These women—senior vice presidents at tech companies, CEOs, computer programmers, partners at law firms, nurses, doctors, and more—were performing better in their careers because they had kids, not in spite of them."

When Jennifer Lopez was given an MTV Lifetime Achievement Award at the 2018 Video Music Awards she talked about how having children made her better and stronger in her career. JLo had twins just when she was at the top of the game, but she realized that she needed to work harder *for them* and this took her career to a whole other level. She said: "I knew I had to be better, I had to go higher, I had to be stronger. It was [through] their unconditional love that my career and my whole life become clearer in every way. And now today I stand here stronger and better than ever. So thank you, Max and Emme. There's so much more to do and I know that in my heart the future is so much brighter because of you."

It's speeches like this from women like JLo that help paint a new picture of who a working mom is. This we know for sure: working mom does not = bad mom.

This myth that just because a woman has kids means she's

disengaged or not committed is just plain wrong. Raising toddlers and teenagers prepares you to deal with coworkers' emotional roller coasters and your boss's psychological tactics. Nothing seems all that stressful after you've experienced rushing your kids to the emergency room. Or having that baby in the first place. It puts work into perspective; it puts life into perspective.

That said, despite how hard they work or systems they put in place, the workplace is behind in evolving to appreciate those efforts. There shouldn't be a bull's-eye on her back. The reality is that unconscious bias training in the workplace around motherhood is very limited. Women are promoted at slower rates than men, paid less, *and* they're also paid less than women without children—a Harvard-reviewed study of hiring practices found that mothers were being offered $11,000 less in starting salary, on average. That same report noted that mothers were significantly less likely to be recommended for a job and were assumed to be "inherently less competent and less committed." It's total BS.

You will need to prepare to meet these realities as you transition to being a mother at work, whether it's people you work with directly, or partners or clients or customers. You will need to prepare to ask for more (knowing this isn't always received well), potentially confront them head-on, create systems that work for you, and if possible, work for change on behalf of other women.

Future Focused

Financial expert Farnoosh Torabi looks at continuing to work as an investment in your career, in yourself, in your finances, in your future. "The return on investment, even if you're at a deficit from child-care costs, will come," says Torabi. "Child-care expenses are a short-term thing. We're willing to take out $80,000 in student loans for our careers but not that equal amount to cover child care?" Throwing your hands up because day care is too expensive is "unfinished math," says Torabi. As we mentioned in chapter 2, the future financial losses from working cannot be underestimated. Your income is helping to cover your family's well-being and to secure your children's future.

Your role as a working mom also has a direct impact on your children's ambitions. Don't downplay your successes but instead be proud of working outside the home. Not only are you a role model for young professional women, but you are the role models for our sons and daughters. "It's important that my kids see me as equally as ambitious and intelligent as their dad," says Emily Hill. "They should understand that I have a world outside of them to also give them an understanding of female potential for leadership." Seeing is believing.

In fact, a Harvard Business School study by Kathleen L. McGinn found that women whose moms worked outside the home are more likely to have jobs themselves, are more likely to hold supervisory responsibility at those jobs, and earn higher wages than women whose mothers stayed home full-time. Men raised by working mothers are more likely to contribute to household chores and spend more time caring for family members. And the findings hold true across twenty-four countries. "There are very few things, that we know of, that have such a clear effect on gender inequality as being raised by a working mother," says McGinn.

McGinn's research also found that kids of working parents are just as happy as kids of stay-at-home moms. Read that sentence again. Your kids will be fine. Own your career. And be prepared for common working-parent pitfalls (stress, guilt, overcommitting)— really pitfalls for any parent, whether you're coming off that first maternity leave or managing two middle schoolers—coming your way. Here's how to set yourself up for success.

1. **Hire the child care you need.**

    You are far from replaceable, but you need a good number two, whether it's a private caregiver, family member, or day care. Adding more loving adults to your child's life is just that—adding love. Take the time to find the right fit—it will bring you untold peace of mind. It's impossible to be your best at work when you are worried about who is with your children. Focus on what's most important for your kids at the moment: someone who has a lot of energy, someone who can help with homework, a day care that doubles as preschool. Also, think about who can help take some worry off your plate: someone who can really manage the household and deal with utility workers; someone who is social enough to set up playdates on her own for the kids; or someone who knows how to make healthy, kid-friendly food. Kids can benefit from having multiple caretakers and learning the various rules and expectations of their parents, grandparents, and babysitters.

    One note: If you're on your first maternity leave and you don't already have a child-care provider, this "to-do" item feels completely overwhelming. But if you've decided to return after leave—and 73 percent of women do—make the most of your break and don't let your lack of child care take over your every thought. Enjoy this time with your babe—it will work out.

2. **Prioritize what's important to your family.**

    Think about where your presence is most valued: to you, to your kids, and to your partner. Talk to your family and ask them: Is it more important to be home for breakfast or play time before bed? In an ideal world, when do they *really* want you to be there? Soccer practice or homework time? School drop-off or field trips? If your kids are really young, ask yourself where you want to be.

Teens want their parents to be flowerpots, the *Wall Street Journal* reported: there if they need them but not helicoptering or bugging them. Teenagers need coaching, support, good examples, and most of all understanding. All things any parent can do, whether working or not.

Most school schedules still cater to nonworking parents. You're going to find yourself juggling constantly to try to be there for things that seem necessary like the first day of school or the Halloween parade, but don't let societal norms about when parents "should" be at school stress you out. Mom shaming has no role at the talent show. And know that many women will have your back. We have both been incredibly grateful for the moms and dads who send videos, photos, and texts when we've missed big moments at the school. If you can, try to plan for and take time off around the events that are most important to you and your child (prepare for the fact that your kids will think the entire summer is critical, so wear your parent hat in these moments!). If you can't, know that these intervals will be short-lived.

One tactic: look for opportunities for mom-at-school face time that fits your schedule, like a volunteer slot before school one day or helping out with an evening talent show. "A lot of my mom friends are very involved at my kids' school," says Meredith Weintraub, an executive producer. "My kids often ask me why I can't be there as much, which does bum me out. So I try to take a day off when my work schedule is a little less crazy to join a field trip each school year." If there's a monthly Monday Girl Scout meeting, for instance, try to block that time on your work schedule. If you simply can't, your best strategy is to set expectations with your kids. Communication is key.

3. **Learn to say no.**

    The ramification of prioritizing is having to say no to things. It's a simple two-letter word, but often one of the hardest to say. The reason? We have a natural inclination to avoid rejecting people, says Vanessa Bohns, an assistant professor of management sciences at Cornell. Her research found that humans have fundamental motivation to stay connected to other people and by saying no we are afraid people will think poorly of us.

    The guilt of saying no is an ongoing, lifelong challenge, one that can be tough to shake, particularly when it involves your children. "No, you cannot go to bed without brushing your teeth," is easy to say without guilt, but "No, I cannot run the bake sale" is harder because you know you're letting someone down.

    I realized I had said yes to too many things when a low tire was enough of an excuse to cancel plans to go to a conference that I knew I should attend, Stacey says. A low tire! It was a wake-up call that I needed to learn a different approach to what I was saying yes to.

    Career coach Laurie Palau of simply B organized offers these strategies to help anyone say no without guilt:

- Realize that it's not permanent. Saying no right now doesn't mean no forever.
- Provide an alternative solution. For example, if someone asks you to chair a committee and you're overextended, suggest someone else who might be a good fit, or offer what time you do have to give.

- It's not personal. When you say no to an opportunity it's different than rejecting the person.
- Be honest. People value honesty and transparency over frustration and martyrdom any day of the week!

The key is to be strategic about what you do let onto your calendar. "I can't do last minute because so much of my week is accounted for with work," says TV producer Lynn McTeague. "And I've had to get comfortable saying no when I have too much on my plate." Setting boundaries is essential to avoiding that panicky feeling of needing to be in a million places at once and praying that someone cancels.

4. **Own your schedule.**
    At work, there is going to be a tug between your desire to go home versus attending events that could advance your career. First, if you haven't already, write down your quarterly career goals. Maybe it's bringing in new business, getting new public speaking gigs, or gaining more visibility at the office. When you're invited to something after work, ask yourself, does this event align with my goals? If yes, it might be worth your time. If not, decline the invite graciously. For those in client-facing roles, where you're wining and dining most nights, or if you find yourself saying "yes, it does align with my goals" quite often, try to put additional parameters around your schedule. If you stay late one day, leave early the next. Or devote Tuesdays and Thursdays to networking. Structure will give you a semblance of control.

    One idea: Leave loudly. It's the act of *not* sneaking out or apologizing for leaving the office at 5 p.m. You just go. It makes the statement that you shouldn't be penalized for owning your schedule. Unfortunately, it's easier for men and more confident senior leaders to embrace this and not feel judged, but a technology-enabled workforce and demand from millennials for a better work-life blend is shifting the norm. Be honest about what you need. You're not mailing it in; if anything you're making yourself a happier, more productive employee. Most day cares close by 6 p.m. The reality is you are probably working during your commute, *and* logging on again once the kids are asleep. But you're helping shift the perception that taking a break from 5 to 8 p.m. to be with your family is a bad thing. Workplaces need to understand and value this time. Women need to not be afraid to take it.

Also, sometimes saying less is more. Men, who generally are looked upon with support when they say they have to leave for something kid related (isn't that wonderful, he's such a good dad), employ the don't-ask, don't-tell method. They leave when they need to and no one says a word. Women, on the other hand, tend to seek permission and are looked down upon when they say they're leaving to pick up a kid (go figure).

5.   Overcommunicate with your kids.

Kids like structure. As they get older, going to work gets harder because they're actually vocalizing the fact they don't want you to leave. Be candid with your kids. Don't over-promise or say that you will "try" to attend something. That can only lead to potential disappointment. Instead, explain to them why you can't attend an event or why you have to work—keep it positive and focused on the satisfaction you have in contributing to your family and the world. "I tell my kids that I really love my job, and that if I'm going to spend so much time away from them, I've made the decision that my job needs to be worth it—and I think it is," says Meredith Weintraub. "I use that conversation as an opportunity to talk to them about finding something they feel really passionate about, something they'll love, when they get older." Talk to your children about what you do for work, why it interests you, and how it's important to find what drives you outside of the comfort of your family.

Also, help them to understand your work schedule so they know what to expect each day. For littles, you can buy a paper calendar and write out the days you will be at work. For families like Jen's, who have two working parents who both travel, three different school schedules, and three different kids' activity schedules, a shared Google calendar has saved their lives. "Even my eight-year-old has his own Gmail account so he can be more responsible with his schedule," she says. "It helps our family communicate better, coordinate car-pool needs, and mitigate potential conflicts. David and I both have a rule that we can't plan a work trip without first checking the calendar. If it's not on the calendar, it doesn't exist." A shared digital calendar has indeed been known to stave off many fights in every household.

6. Onboard people to help

We can't do this alone. The most important task: bring other people on board. This can include your spouse or partner, a grandparent, a babysitter, etc. If you're married, this may be a time to discuss if your spouse could take on the bulk of the parenting role. Many successful women (and men) have a spouse who turns the career dial down for a bit. Or a partner with a more flexible schedule. If you're a solo parent, this means engaging your network of friends and caregivers.

Ian, a former stockbroker, has been home with his kids since his oldest was sixteen months (she's nine now) so his wife, Alicia, could focus on work. Alicia always knew she wanted to work—she was driven and passionate about her career. They discussed this well before having kids. When their daughter was around one year old, Alicia found out she was pregnant again. The surprises didn't end: their nanny's visa was up and she had to go back to Brazil, and business for Ian, who was working on the floor of the New York Stock Exchange, was flatlining. "It was the perfect storm," Ian says. "There was no question that Alicia would keep working. She wanted to. I could see that the future wasn't looking as bright for my business so we decided that I would try staying home with the kids." Now, as a family of five, they've had to make some sacrifices, but it works for them. And Ian loves it.

If you are both working, require your partner to be in the loop and share responsibilities for the kids. It shouldn't be all on you. It can't be all on you. Ask your partner for help—sometimes you have to spell it out. Most don't have mind-reading superpowers. Tiffany Dufu addresses this in her book, *Drop the Ball*. Dufu says most of us have a tendency toward imaginary delegation—that syndrome of getting mad when someone doesn't do what you think they should have just *known* to do (like empty the dishwasher), but you never actually asked them to do it. Sometimes you have to point it out and ask. We both do this. What woman doesn't? It's the good ol' "honey do" list and it's brilliant.

Get ready to communicate about these facts of life. Who's going to handle things like:

- doctor's appointments
- grocery shopping
- school/activity sign-ups
- school volunteering
- being present without work distractions

Divide and conquer based on what you both like to do—not based on what is traditionally deemed "women's work." You don't like to cook? Don't stress about it. Ruth Bader Ginsburg doesn't cook—and we're pretty sure that's not going to be noted on her tombstone. RBG had a young daughter when she was one of only eight women who attended Harvard Law School in the 1950s. She didn't get a lot of sleep and worked in the middle of the night, but she made her dreams happen. And she didn't waste her time or energy worrying about what others thought of her. She had a supportive husband who did not require her to be a perfect housewife. If RBG could do this in a time when women held mostly administrative roles in the workplace, we can make it happen for ourselves today.

If you don't have a partner, finding a company that "gets it" will be critical. Sanam Saaber, a single mother of twins and general counsel at a software company, told us how the culture there allowed for her to comfortably leave a big meeting on the spot when her son had a high fever. "Don't be afraid to speak up about what you need to make your life work," she says. "The biggest thing I do to set boundaries is simply telling people when something doesn't work for me and offering an alternative."

7. Rally your other support system.

As more women have children in their forties, there's a good chance the grandparents are in their seventies and possibly not as spritely as they once were. This is why more and more women are turning to a network of friends for support. We both have relied on the kindness of our more available friends to carpool when we're in a bind, or even when we're not. Embrace your stay-at-home/part-time mom friends. Don't be too proud to ask a friend for a favor. A text about how your kid is doing at the game you're missing has the power to eliminate guilt and change your mood. You don't have to act like you have everything together all the time.

Frankly, for women as a whole to move forward, we need to stop judging each other's career decisions and help each other out. Tiffany Dufu says, "We are all working mothers. Some of us get paid and some of us don't. The latter are the women who spend a lot of time outside the home doing everything from volunteering to grocery shopping to shuttling kids around—including mine. Nonpaid working moms are an important part of my village and I wouldn't be able to make a difference in the world without them."

Give back to your village, too. If Sara drives your son to soccer practice every week, how are you helping her out? Can you reciprocate on the weekends? Drive when you are available? Or maybe there's something else you can do that doesn't just have to be a playdate exchange. Maybe you can look at someone's resume. Get her tickets to a concert. Send her flowers. Treat these relationships like the valuable assets that they are.

8. **Create your own power circle.**

We need to help women find the collective power of their voices. I regret not reaching out to women in a similar position earlier in my career and cultivating my own girls' club at work, Jen says. I realize this now, as younger women at my firm are reaching out to me for advice. If I had established my own network to talk about what was going on in my head, I may have given myself more career choices instead of simply quitting. Men are very comfortable with giving references for one another, recommending each other for jobs, sponsoring and supporting one another. Women are getting better at this.

Pamela Ryckman, author of *Stiletto Network*, speaks of the rise of the powerful women's network across the country, where ambitious women are coming together to help one another create a more female-friendly world. It's happening at lunch dates, at employee resource groups, and at the playground. Organizations like Lean In, Dufu's the Cru, Ellevate, Watermark, the Wing, Female Quotient, and countless women's networking groups are catalyzing efforts.

Just start somewhere to connect with professionals who can understand what you're dealing with as a working parent. And your supporters don't have to be limited to women—anyone who understands what it's like to be a working parent can be an ally. Build a network of people that get you; that understand where you're going and what you're going through. Start a women's initiative group at your company if they don't have one.

9. Prioritize self-care.

There will be plenty of things out of your control—sick kids, having to stay at work late—so try to stay ahead of the things that *are* in your control. If possible, set up automatic bill pay, set calendar reminders to buy family birthday presents, have your groceries delivered every weekend, and have dog food and diapers auto-shipped. Modern-day technology is a lifesaver for any parent and can give you tiny pockets of time back.

The Fringe Hours, by Jessica Turner, presents the concept that there are moments throughout the day that are underused and when you find them and capitalize on them, you will bring more happiness to your life. For Jessica, it's the early morning hours before her kids wake up that she "invests in herself" and takes time to write or bake. For others, it might be reading a chapter while waiting on line for lunch or calling a friend on your commute (it takes the average worker twenty-six minutes to travel to work, according to the U.S. Census Bureau).

It's crucial to carve out time for yourself. Easier said than done, we know, but self-care isn't just a buzzword. It's vital for your well-being and your career to keep your brain active and alive. A recent Gallup study reports that two-thirds of employees reported feeling burned out at work and that employees who experience burnout are more likely to take a sick day, are less confident and engaged in their work, and are 2.6 times as likely to leave their current employer. Two of the five main contributors to burnout? Unmanageable workload and unreasonable time pressures.

Author and entrepreneur Randi Zuckerberg says she, like most of us, is constantly reacting to other people's priorities and that her to-do list became quickly composed of what emails were coming in or who was texting her. In Randi's book, *Pick Three: You Can Have It All, Just Not Every Day*, she says you need to choose three priorities for every day, whether it's Family, Fitness, Friends/Fun, Work, or Sleep. "You can't squeeze in four," she says. "Those priorities can change every day, though. That's how you get back control." We love this concept of giving yourself permission to not do it all, but make it your own: Work and Family will most likely always be in your daily priorities—you can't ignore those categories! But create self-care categories that are personal and inspiring to you, for example, like Culture, Nature, Fitness, Friends, Learning. Try to put these on top of your list at least two days a week.

Part of the challenge is silencing your inner critic that self-care = being selfish. Sometimes that voice in your head is just plain wrong. Don't let it take over your thoughts or misconstrue other's intentions. Après coach Rosie Guagliardo of InnerBrilliance Coaching suggests naming your inner critic to silence it once it starts. She calls hers "Mean Old Nonnie."

One woman told us that her mother-in-law once said to her, "I am really impressed that you manage to take time for yourself." The woman's knee-jerk reaction was that this was a passive-aggressive dig about her role as a mom (or lack thereof), but she quickly realized that her MIL truly meant it. Too often, we feel guilty for spending forty-five minutes exercising or fifteen minutes meditating when we haven't seen our kids all day, but taking care of your physical and mental needs will make you a more relaxed, rested mom.

The point is to make time for what makes you happy or what you know you need to feel good about yourself. Your kids won't remember that you snuck off to get a manicure and missed watching *Star Wars* with them.

10. Give up on failure and guilt.

Most women we spoke to feel that they're always failing at some part of their life, whether it's work, home, marriage, or friendships. But how do you currently define failure? Missing a music class? Skipping a happy-hour event? Not volunteering at school? Not reading the book club book? Not getting to in-box zero? Mom burnout is real. Striving for a world of false perfection where you are wildly successful at work, there for every important kid event, finish all your to-dos, and have a circle of best friends is fruitless.

Reshma Saujani, founder of Girls Who Code, struck a nerve with her 2016 TED talk imploring the world to teach girls bravery, not perfection. After the talk, her in-box was flooded with emails of gratitude for releasing women from unrealistic expectations. In her book *Brave, Not Perfect*, Saujani writes: "Some of the emails made me cry as I read how women and girls felt tyrannized by perfectionism: 'When I make a mistake or let someone down, I beat myself up for days,' one woman said. 'It's all I can think about.' Another wrote, 'Everyone thinks I'm this person who has everything under control . . . if they only knew how hard I work to look that way and how afraid I am that someone will see the mess that I really am.'"

Guilt. It's a loaded word. Not all working parents have it, but for the ones that do, it can usurp your mind, body, and career. Here are three rules to let it go.

Rule #1: Take it easy on yourself.

A 2017 Pew study shows that 43 percent of full-time working mothers think they don't spend enough time with their children. But, for most of the history of the world, women did not sit on the floor and play Legos with their kids all day. They were baking, washing clothing, cooking, and cleaning. Modern women also devote more time to child care than our predecessors, from 14 hours a week in 2016 compared to 10 hours in 1965. Yes, those numbers seem ridiculously low, especially when it feels like you're changing diapers and worrying about them 24/7, but it's 14 hours of uninterrupted time with your child—not cooking, cleaning, multitasking, running errands, watching TV. And it's okay to admit you don't love that time.

There are days you will feel like a fabulous mom and a terrible employee and other days you feel like a terrible mom and a fabulous employee, and that's normal. Focusing your energy on where it's most needed at that moment (a sick kid, a demanding client) is a smart strategy. Stop the pursuit of perfection. It's a losing battle.

Cut yourself some slack at work, too. In most fields, growth and salary increases happen more quickly when you change positions and companies, but there is a level of comfort, convenience, and leniency that exists when you've already proven yourself. "I have forfeited quick growth to embrace all the benefits that are offered as a respected, loyal employee," says Lynn McTeague. "I take my vacation days, work remotely one day per week, and don't think twice when I'm late due to a school concert or parent-teacher meeting." Own your schedule with no guilt.

Now, even being comfortable with your decision doesn't mean there won't be struggles. You will doubt it on bad days and be grateful on good days. When you successfully nail a presentation, order a birthday present for your mother-in-law, and get home in time for dinner—you'll be on a high. The next day, when you're in meeting purgatory, forget you were in charge of carpool, have no food in the fridge, and are in commuting hell—you're going to raise a fist to the career gods. But you will survive. You will thrive.

Rule #2: Stop comparing yourself to others.

The grass always seems greener for other moms. Working moms look longingly at the ones heading off to grab a cup of coffee to-gether, and career-break moms look longingly at the well-dressed woman heading off to an important meeting.

It's natural to feel envious of the moms who are home with their kids—especially when you see the strong bonds formed with other moms in their situations. The reality is those moms (and their kids) spend more time together, whether at playdates, at the park, wherever. And it can leave you feeling like an outsider. "I am sometimes jealous of the relationships my mommy friends have with one another," one woman told us. "They are together all the time so they know one another better than they know me." It can be difficult to "break in" to the group—and sometimes this can make it harder for your kids to break in as well.

Creating a village of friends is crucial for any woman, and sometimes this takes time. It's like freshman year of college. Remember when everyone would go out during orientation in groups of twenty or more and then they slowly dwindled down? That's what happens when making adult friends, too. While you most likely don't have a ton of free time to grab a cup of coffee during the day, reach out to someone on the weekends. Be proactive about playdates for when you are available.

According to Pew research, most parents care what others in their community think of their parenting skills. About half (52 percent) of mothers and fathers surveyed said it matters *a lot* to them that their friends see them as a good parent. And most moms we talk to say they like to give the impression that their lives are under control—that they will only share the true messy details with their closest friends. That facade is working. Sixty-two percent of working mothers believe other parents have an easier time accomplishing everyday tasks, according to a Care.com survey. Yes, there is the mom who makes adorable cupcakes for the bake sale, but you never know what goes on behind closed doors. Every mom has her own story. And everyone needs to respect those stories.

Yet contempt for one another's personal choices is prevalent. According to the 2017 C. S. Mott Children's Hospital National Poll on Children's Health, 61 percent of mothers with kids under the age of five have admitted to being criticized over their parenting decisions: how their kids ate, how long they slept, their safety.

Where exactly does this come from? Is it insecurity? Envy? "I think that mom shaming is a psychological reaction to the feelings of pressure and chaos that are natural in motherhood," Dr. Alexandra Sacks told Romper. If you don't feel like you have it all together, you're quick to point out the faults in others to make yourself feel better.

One mom told us younger women ask her if it's hard for her to bond with her kids because she travels so much. Jaw-dropping, yes, but God love her, she uses it as a teaching moment to share how she does. Try to be a guide for other women; talk with women about how you manage it (or how you don't). You can make a difference, too.

Rule #3: Remember your motivation.

By working, you're making the decision to invest in your (and your family's) future. "To me, that's critical for the stability of our family, which helps outweigh the guilt," says Emily Hill. Providing for your family is not a choice, it's a necessity.

Another reason you work is that you love what you do and it brings you some amount of fulfillment. And that makes you a better mom. Self-acceptance is incredibly important. If you're the person who's happy working, don't beat yourself up over it. That's Jen. She knows it about herself. Stacey is happiest when she owns her schedule. Not everyone is the same and that is okay. These are lessons we're passing along to our children.

No Decision Is Final

Take a regular gut check. Is it still worth it? Are you still motivated? Are you being rewarded?

Some women feel trapped by the decision to stay. "Despite

every moment of doubt, I never quit," one woman told us. "Seeing the way time out of the workforce can become a black mark for other women in my industry was enough to make me stick it out through the tough times, even when I was really unhappy." Just remember, nothing is permanent.

If you're feeling really overwhelmed and burned out, take a few personal days or look into a short-term sabbatical program. Several companies offer long-term employees (you've been there at least four years or so) this option—we see it in corporations where employees tend to have long track records like Chevron, BP, Cigna Healthcare, Aetna, Kaiser, Genentech, PwC. Deloitte, for instance, offers two sabbatical options: The first is one month unpaid to do anything you desire, whether it's to travel or devote yourself to real self-care time. It's like hitting a pause button, and it might be just what you need. The second is a three- to six-month sabbatical in which you are paid at 40 percent of your base salary. For the latter, you need to show the company how you will use this time to pursue external career development opportunities or volunteer experiences.

You may find yourself wanting to reevaluate your career choices when your kids are in elementary school or middle school. "As my kids have gotten older some things have gotten easier, but many things have gotten more difficult," says Amy Glazer, development director for a nonprofit. "When you have a baby most of what you 'miss' is for you—the mom. In grade school, children realize that you are not at pickup, or can't come in to volunteer for lunch. Then, in middle school and high school, sometimes you need to be available to listen, give support or advice. Balancing all of this and a career is very challenging." Feel comfort in the knowledge that your career will go through phases just like your children do: dialed up, down, or sparking a steady flame.

Lisa quit her job at a major tech company when her girls were six and eight. She had felt that she hit a plateau at work and that her career ambitions were not compatible with the type of mother she wanted to be. She pivoted from sales to a communications role to ease the traveling requirements. "But it still wasn't quite working for me." It was agonizing to make the decision to leave, Lisa says, but in the end she knew what she really wanted to do (write and spend more time with her kids) wasn't even the same as what she wanted when her kids were born. Circumstances change. Desires change. Now Lisa is back to working full-time.

When you leave the workforce later, there is certainly less opt-out doubt. Women who have done this say they have put in their time and now are ready for the next chapter: volunteering more, spending time with the kids, starting a business, or simply enjoying the chance to clear their head and hit reset.

WHEN YOUR MATERNITY LEAVE ENDS

It's normal to feel anxious when your maternity leave comes to an end. Depending on the length of your break, you may still be healing physically and struggling emotionally. Questions abound: How will I handle this? Do I want to go back? Is my job in jeopardy? Am I going to pump? Where? Here's how to prepare for your return.

1. **Don't make any big decisions.** We do caution that if you're considering a break as your maternity leave is coming to an end versus having made the decision long ago, that you do go back to work, even for a short period of time. You can't know what it's like until you get there, and you may love it, or it may make your decision all that much easier.

2. **Consider negotiating for more time.** Ask friends and colleagues what they asked for and how the company worked with them. You'll likely be able to max out your paid vacation and sick time as well. Also, investigate your partner's leave time. You will be surprised at the relief it will give you to know another parent is home with the baby while you are at work and it will help relieve some of the stress of going back.

3. **Confirm your return date with HR and your boss.** Try to return midweek—your reentry will feel less daunting. One woman we know came back a week earlier than she told her clients so she could catch up and get a handle on everything before she needed to be present for them. Fill out any paperwork necessary to ensure you start getting paid again.

4. **If you want to breastfeed, explore options.** Ask about provisions and policies on pump rooms and any other benefits for breastfeeding moms. Before you return to work, make sure your baby is adjusted to bottle feedings.

5. **Practice being away.** Before returning to work, practice with your care providers and gradually increase the time apart from your baby and also to get the baby physically comfortable with the surroundings and care providers.

6. **Send an update to your team.** Let them know when you will be returning as well and how you want to catch up with each of them individually. Think about your preferences: it can be overwhelming to have a packed schedule on day one, but it also might take your mind off baby.

7. **Know it's okay to cry.** This most likely will go one of two ways. Day one will be really tough or you're truly ready to go back and are somewhat relieved and you feel guilty. In either situation, go for a walk, collect yourself, and know everyone feels that way.

8. **Ease yourself back in.** Go on a listening tour to find out what's been happening since you were gone. Ask people where you are most needed right now.

9. **Hire a coach.** Yes, there is such a thing as a maternity leave coach and they are truly experts in helping women ease their way back into the workplace and navigate the emotions and logistics of returning to your job after baby.

HOW COMPANIES CAN SHINE:
Engage and commit to those who stay.

While companies talk a big game about putting more women into leadership positions, data from reports like Lean In and McKinsey & Company's annual Women in the Workplace shows that there has been little to no improvement, particularly as you move up the ranks toward the executive suite. When a woman returns from maternity leave—or is at a crossroads when family life is simply too overwhelming—there is tremendous opportunity for a company to begin a long partnership with her. It benefits everyone: Companies with greater gender diversity have been shown to exhibit a stronger growth culture and propensity for new solutions and innovation, are 1.7 times more likely to have strong leadership, and are 1.4 times more likely to have sustained profitable growth. Open the dialogue. Listen. Communicate. Some ideas:

1. **Boost child-care options.** Can you ease the cost and demands of child care, a major factor in driving women out of the workforce? Offer a child-care stipend, child-care FSA, or backup child-care options that are actually useful, like access to UrbanSitter, Care.com, or BrightHorizons. Consider a kids' room where older kids can come and do homework after school. Or, go big: while expensive, child care on site can be a game changer for parents. Nike offers a full on-site day care in its Oregon headquarters, as do Disney Parks, Clif Bar, Genentech, Patagonia, General Mills, SAS Institute, and Goldman Sachs.

2. **Help parents manage the household.** It's the "small" projects or important chores that tend to consume (and overwhelm) working parents. Many women we spoke to, like HR executive Elizabeth Scott, said if there was an employee assistance program to handle this type of mental labor, they could focus on work. Many companies like Accenture, American Express, and EY offer some level of concierge service that can take on these types of tasks. Wellthy, for instance, has a program that will vet nannies, hire a house manager, and even find caretakers for elderly parents. Separately, you can offer classes on time management and how to create an equal partner household. Mothers's groups and Women in Leadership groups play a big role at this time.

3. **Coach them for success.** What are you doing to help move women up the ladder? Women need midcareer mentors and

career coaches. Think about continuing education opportunities and offering tuition reimbursement or online courses for those employees who are committed to improving. Offer opportunities for women to communicate with each other and learn from each other during this stage of career and life.

CHAPTER 4

THE CASE FOR TAKING A BREAK

Am I all out?

There is a stereotype of a woman who steps out of the workforce—that she's not ambitious, that she's rich and has a hugely successful partner, that she's sipping rosé all day in workout pants while shopping at Target. We know this isn't true. You know this isn't true. There's a misconception that it's only a privileged few who are making this decision.

It's also a terribly antiquated perspective and, we'll argue, subjugates women in a way that perpetuates stereotypes that lead to conscious and unconscious bias, unequal pay, fewer promotions, and a sidelined "shadow" talent pool.

It's also inaccurate. A 2017 Brookings Institution report tells us: "After 2000, we see that women of all education groups experienced a decline in [labor force] participation—with the most notable decline for those with less education, including some college or less, and the least dramatic for those with a bachelor's degree or higher, similar to what we observe among prime-age men."

"Taking a break" for some might not feel exactly like a break, but rather a time of "being pushed out" by work infrastructures that don't work—for example, hourly workers who can't predict a schedule and thus can't find child care.

We know this to be true: taking a career break does not lessen your ability and talent to contribute to the workforce in the future and should never be viewed as a character flaw when applying for a job. The concept of coming and going from the workplace should be normalized and expected, rather than unusual and unexpected.

Moreover, the thousands of women we speak to about career breaks and coming back from one *are* ambitious. They're at every socioeconomic level and have made a decision to focus on family. They admit they've felt the financial ramifications of the decision, and they're frustrated that their male counterparts haven't been faced with the same career setbacks. They also clearly see the mountain many climb to get back in.

No woman's story for why she took a break is the same. I really loved my job, Stacey says. I interviewed Jeff Bezos and Elon Musk, produced interviews with Bill Gates, learned about young start-up companies, spoke to economists about the real estate market, rode in cutting-edge cars, and traveled to cool places to see and talk to people about interesting topics. And I got to be on camera and share what I learned with others! It was all seamless until it wasn't.

Some women we talked to were caught off guard by the decision, whether it was surprise by how much they wanted to be with their baby ("I don't care if we eat mac 'n' cheese every night, I want to stay home with her," one woman told her husband) or surprise by the inflexibility of their workplaces. There are those who knew they wanted to take a break and saved up for this period in life, and still others whose spouse or culture expected that they would quit to caregive. It's imperative not to assume, and also to respect choices, not penalize them.

In the same way that women choose to continue working (largely in a system that works against them), we need to empower women who decide to step back. No, you did not fail at your career—you made the best decision for you and your family, for now. This is not necessarily forever, so embrace the moment.

Taking a career break can be an incredible gift. It is a decision and transition to go into with eyes wide open, of course. Look at a career reprieve as an opportunity to be really present in this specific phase of your life, whether you are making a conscious choice or feel backed into a financial corner.

And just as you get excited about being free of the day-to-day, know that the path ahead, while fun, certainly isn't challenge-free. Women and men both admit that staying home with the kids can be "a thousand times harder than going to work." There are no lunch breaks, you're at the whim of tiny tyrants, and you have to break into the new parent circles. It's a new set of social cues to understand. Vast swaths of the day are devoted to play, cleaning, cooking, and planning. It can be boring and stressful, so as much as you can, take a moment to look at what you will gain by being free of the daily work grind: time to breathe and time to spend with your children. And as any parent knows, the older the children get, the faster the years clip by.

Seven years. That's how long my break was, Jen says. Seven years in which I built an infrastructure around my life at home. In that time I made an incredible group of friends and created a solid village for my family. I feel so lucky I had the time to do this. But I didn't always handle it well because, let's face it, it is a big adjustment going from the fast-paced corporate world to the much slower-paced world of toddlers. Sometimes I felt like I was in the movie *Groundhog Day*; many days felt the same to me. But I also loved the time away from work. I was cooking more, focusing on my health. And now, as I'm back in the workforce, I have these new skills, healthy habits, and a support system that I can rely on when I need help, which is more often than you may think. I also have a real appreciation for just how hard it is to be a stay-at-home mom. It is, quite frankly, the most difficult job in the world.

Quitting is also a chance to snub the system that's ultimately very rigged against you—women aren't paid the same, they're lucky to have flexible hours, as most don't, and they aren't promoted at the same rate. You're lucky if you get paid leave. Child care is expensive. Work culture is essentially 24/7. The ability to work and check email at any given hour creates an internal struggle about setting work and family boundaries.

Stepping away from the day-to-day grind, and experiencing life in and out of the workforce, grants you a new perspective on your whole career continuum and helps you figure out your walk-away points—namely, what do you most value in your job, what would make you come back, and what's just not worth it anymore? Ironically, while your confidence will ebb and flow during this time, it does lead to a stronger sense of one's own career ideals.

Time can indeed lead to new opportunities. You never know what is going to come from making such a big change. One former financial analyst told us she was most surprised that quitting "would liberate me to consider different career options than before. Quitting to be a mom really burst open the notion that I had to stay on some self-imposed, narrow track. It made me think bigger picture and redefine my idea of success."

Finding yourself, discovering new passions, creating roots in your town, being with your kids: there are a myriad of benefits that come with quitting, but there are challenges, too. "I am happy I took a break when I did and had the opportunity to spend that time with my kids—it's time you don't get back," says Joy, who works in corporate communications. "I went on to have a third daughter and got more involved in the school and community because I was physically present. My 'break' lasted about eight years. I am grateful for that time, but it did put a significant financial strain on us." Money stress can grow high when moving from two incomes to one. The fastest way to temper it? Plan and save for this time period in advance as best you can.

How to Save for a Career Break

Forty-two percent of married millennials and 37 percent of un-married millennials are very clear that they plan to interrupt their career for family, according to a survey of Harvard Business School alumni. Having that intention grants you time to save for lost salary years, which is incredibly freeing. Farnoosh Torabi, host of the *So Money* podcast, said, "I'm able to say it's the choices I made prior to having kids to create a savings foundation that allowed me to not feel trapped." The money you put in a midca-reer sabbatical fund (or whatever you wish to call it) can be used during your break to contribute to the household costs even while you're not working. The genius here is that it will ease some of the financial burden of quitting and empower you to not feel like you have to manage everything because you are "being supported" by your spouse.

Ideally, all couples are having conversations about what the dynamics of raising children will look like well before having children. Yes, life changes, circumstances change, emotions change—we know this. But at the core you may have a vision of your future, or strong opinions of your parents' career decisions.

Like Jen, Stacey grew up with the role model of a mother who worked very hard—but starting when she was in the fourth grade. After ten years of staying at home, Stacey's mom, Sherry Delo, built an amazingly successful second career as a financial advisor. She fell into it after someone heard her talking about the stock market at a party and suggested she come in for an interview. She got her CFP and cold-called her way to incredible success, eventually starting her own firm.

My mom got up at 4:30 a.m. most days to get ahead of work and ultimately owned her schedule, Stacey says. I don't ever remember her missing big school events—though I do remember her occasionally peeling into the school parking lot on two wheels to pick us up on time. As a result, I had the good fortune of someone who could help me look ahead and also not feel like my choices would define me for long periods of time. Luckily, she could also talk me through the financials of shifting to a more flexible opportunity to be with children.

If one of you wants to take a break, save for this grace period just as you would any other financial goal like retirement or a new house. "Saving for a career break is saving for your future, too," says Sherry. Here's how to do it: Use the guidelines in chapter 2 to approximate how much you'll need to save to cover your expenses. Ideally, you're saving as much as you can. If you can save 50 percent of your current salary, you will be setting yourself up for less financial stress during your break, but any extra money you can put aside for every year you think you might be out of the workforce will ease the transition to a one-income family.

If you have time on your side, open an investment account where you could potentially earn a 5 to 7 percent return on stocks and bonds—for example, a balanced (65 percent stock, 35 percent bonds) mutual fund—instead of 2 to 3 percent with a savings account. If you're looking to grow this fund more rapidly, try to put any bonuses or cash gifts you receive into the account. Then consider lowering your 401(k) contributions. Contribute to the point that earns a corporate match, if available. "That's free money," says Sherry. But divert the rest to yourself. "People are so fixated on saving for retirement, but they're not setting themselves up to be financially sound in all the years leading up to that," says Sherry. "If it turns out that for whatever reason you don't stop working, you will have a tremendous investment and savings account for a rainy day."

It's never too late to start saving. If you're pregnant with your first and considering not returning from maternity leave, be more aggressive about putting away your salary. If you have two young kids and need a break, give yourself as much time as you can to save some of your salary. Look to budgeting software and communities like You Need a Budget (YNAB) or Mint for advice on how to move from two incomes to one. You don't need millions to do it. Any cushion will help ease the financial strain, and give you more clarity and freedom to make decisions in the absence of money.

And when you're ready to go, do it right.

How to Quit Gracefully

When you decide to tell your employer you're leaving, how you handle yourself will be a key factor in your return-to-work path. We can't stress this enough—it is vital to end on a good note. You might be thinking in the moment that this is it, you're never looking back! But you should never underestimate how you might feel in a year, two years, or five years. Look at every place you work as someone whom you will know for the rest of your career. You want them to recommend you; you want to be able to reach out and ask for help later down the road. And even if you know 100 percent you don't want to return to that company, you will most likely need their contacts when you do return to the job market. Here are some other tactical tips:

Quit in person or over the phone if you're remote. This is a no-brainer; it's such an important conversation to have and it's best done as that, a conversation.

Give ample notice. The thing that stresses out employers when an employee quits is not having adequate time to fill a position. While two weeks is technically the standard, since you're not rushing off to a new job, try to give as much notice as you can—or your backup babysitting allows. The benefit to you is that you can also take this time to be proactive and meet with as many of your colleagues as possible to give a proper good-bye (and stay in their good graces!).

Be honest about why you're leaving. Take some key colleagues out to coffee (one at a time) and explain your story. Be candid and don't be afraid to show your vulnerability. Say something like, "I'm leaving and taking a career break. I've never done this before and I am a little nervous—can I keep in touch with you while I'm out?" People appreciate candor and will remember you for it. Again, you never know who you might need to be a touchstone later down the road. Even if you don't actually email that person for two years, you've laid the groundwork.

Work hard. While embarking on a farewell tour is important for your future, you need to also do your job well up until the last day. Work with your boss on a solid transition plan. Offer to train people on what you do. Organize your papers and information and disseminate to anyone who may need it. Leave with a solid reputation.

Ask about return-to-work programs. If you're not already aware of programs or policies at your company, ask about them. Tell HR and your boss that "I love working here, and I know you can't guarantee a position, but can you keep an open mind about me coming back in the future?"

Don't go negative. Even if you're feeling like your employer gave you no choice but to resign—whether it was for unrealistic travel expectations or declining your flexibility proposal—hold your head up high as you leave. If there's an exit interview, don't be afraid to be honest about your disappointment in the lack of parent-friendly policies if that's the case, but remain respectful. You always want to leave the proverbial door open—maybe not at that place if it's a horrible place to work (!)—but your manager might be a good egg and you want to do right by him or her.

Stay in touch. We will repeat this advice over and over again until it seeps into your subconscious. You can be selective, but you need to keep tabs on a few people in your network. Two and a half years after leaving her company to be with her boys, Stacey's sister was invited to a milestone celebration for the start-up. Even though she had to get a sitter and commute two and a half hours for the evening event, she still decided to go. In the end, she came out of the night with potential contract work—opportunity that might not have come if she stayed home. But staying connected isn't just about priming yourself for an eventual return. Many women we spoke with said they wish they had known how much they'd miss their professional friendships. For many of us, these are the people you spend the bulk of your days with and truly become your closest friends and allies. They're your work family! Don't underestimate how easy it can be to fall out of touch—make a plan to stay connected, whether it's a monthly lunch or even a texting date.

HOW TO DISCUSS THE DECISION TO QUIT WITH YOUR PARTNER

The best approach is to include your partner in your decision-making process and discuss all the reasons and questions we tackled in chapter 2, but if your partner is still nervous or hesitant about the final decision, here are Après career coach Julie Houghton's tips regarding how to have a healthier, more productive conversation.

1. **Make your partner feel heard.** Validate your partner's fears and admit that this is scary. Simply mirroring back what they're saying can go a long way toward easing some of the tension and concern.

2. **Have a plan and share it.** Your partner might be concerned about how this is all going to work. Discuss it together: Should you commit to a certain savings goal before you quit? What do you plan to do to stay connected with your career to make the transition back easier?

3. **Reiterate why you need this.** Your partner might know how unhappy you are because of how much you talk about it. But really explain why this new path will be better and make a difference in your whole family's lives.

4. **Be thankful.** Tell your partner that you're grateful for any bit of support he or she can offer. Expressing appreciation can go a long way.

Easing the Identity Crisis

Your last day of work can be exhilarating, much like the last day of school. It's a rush; you leave work and it's amazing. You feel like you've eliminated this huge stressful thing in your life. You can have lunch with a friend and not feel like you're playing hooky or the constant pressure to check work emails! You can work out (probably), you can sleep more (maybe), you can enjoy yourself (definitely)!

You're in the honeymoon phase.

But, sadly, the honeymoon does end. The transition from working to not is rife with complications. Going from being with your kids for only a few hours a day, if that, to primary caregiver is a big adjustment. You're going to go through doubts, you're going to lament the fact that you can't eat lunch in peace—or even eat lunch at all; you're going to question who you are and what you just decided to do. You're going to feel like you're losing your identity. Given that women are waiting longer to have children, this identity crisis may feel even more startling because you are further along in your career.

You're going to miss the energy of being around people and potentially dressing for work. You're going to miss workplace strategizing and brainstorms. You'll likely miss people telling you you're doing a good job (positive feedback is a very rare occurrence in parenting!). When Stacey made the decision to scale back, one of her mentors told her it would feel a little like a death, going from pre-kid career self to post-kid career self. Wiping someone's bottom is not the same as killing it in a sales presentation and certainly doesn't leave you feeling ambitious.

The hardest part for me on the days I wasn't working was being able to turn off my sincere interest in contributing at work and feeling sad that the two—my work and my baby—couldn't exist better together at the same time, Stacey says. It was hard to break the habit of checking my phone regularly and I found myself still absorbing every news alert. Years later Stacey met Sabrina Parsons, whose company Palo Alto Software allowed women to bring their babies to work up to the point they were no longer "wearable" as infants. We love the concept of that model because it allows women to not have to choose one path or the other too early. We know exactly how this feels and wish someone had better prepared us for this transition, too.

After spending close to half her career at Google and YouTube (nearly twelve and a half years), Lisa decided that her career ambitions weren't compatible with the type of mother she wanted to be and made the decision to quit. The first month she took to clear her head. It was a bit of a shock to her system to not think about her work. "The loss of meaning in my days and sense of purpose was not something I was expecting," she says. "So much of my identity was tied up in my career. That said, the time with my girls was awesome and exactly what I had hoped for. It was my time *without* them, while they were in school, that I felt useless. You expect to feel so fulfilled, but it's hard for someone who has focused on her career for nearly twenty years to all of a sudden drop that focus."

Being with little kids all the time is a different kind of exhausting. We all know those "super" moms who make it look fun and easy, all while looking fabulous themselves. But for the rest of us, it's not going to be an Instagram-worthy series. There are meltdowns over buttered toast and internal shaming for yelling more than you wish you had. Guilt will rear its head again, but this time it's guilt for not loving being with your kids 24/7; or guilt about not contributing to the family finances; or that you're getting a manicure; or that you're not finding time to work out even though you should be able to find time to work out now.

It was two years post-quitting when the reality of being a stay-at-home mom settled in, Jen says. I was Grace's mom, I was Henry's mom. I wasn't Jen. I had somehow lost some of my identity. I had to own up to the fact that I wasn't on an extended maternity leave right now—I was a full-time child-care provider and that wasn't jiving with how I saw myself. It was jarring, and I know it is all too common for women who go from the boardroom to the nursery. I used to be the most ambitious person in the room—I wanted that seat at the table and I went after it. I realized that that feeling of being motivated to work toward something, whether it was a promotion, more money, or a pat on the back from my boss, was long gone. I needed to find that person again.

Don't Lose Sight of Yourself

Women are often put in boxes by others—"Mom," "wife," "daughter"—and it is very easy to fall into the trap of allowing yourself to be identified by the box. Throughout your entire motherhood + career tour, it is imperative that you value yourself as an individual first, without any labels. Think back to the time before you had kids and a family, when it was just you figuring out what you wanted out of life. What motivated you? What fulfilled you? When you're stuck in the grind of daily life, and your identity hinges on being the best parent you can be, it can be easy to lose sight of that. Especially since for most of us our sense of self and purpose is wrapped up in work and the external validation and accolades we received there. Write them down and put them in a place where you can refer to them.

Because of this, many women tell us that they find themselves struggling with introducing themselves, conversation topics, and the lack of interpersonal energy from chatting with colleagues. Laura, a television producer, speaks of the identity crisis she faced when she stopped working. At cocktail parties, she was used to being asked about her hit show or any good behind-the-scenes gossip. After a few years, all she felt like she could contribute to the conversation were sleep-training strategies and the best oils for baby eczema. And it took a toll on her self-esteem.

She's not alone. Many women are very self-critical of their decision to take a break, and imagine silent judgment from colleagues or friends who didn't go this route. They're afraid that they're now looked at as a quitter, or a failure to the women's movement. "Until that point, I was a doer, a provider, a 'success story,'" says Gail, a lawyer. "Becoming a stay-at-home mom felt in some ways like surrendering." But, to make this work for you and your family, you need to flip the script in your head to feel confident in your decision, surround yourselves with people who are going to lift you up, and hold on to yourself—even on the really bad days.

Some days are going to be mind-numbingly boring. Others will be amazing, and when they are, give yourself a pat on the back. "I wish I had known that you must be comfortable with not receiving acknowledgment for your work in the way you receive accolades, praise, and money for paid work," says Anu, a human resources analyst. "Staying home is an exercise in selflessness." Be patient and don't take it out on your partner when the praise doesn't come rolling in. That said, when you're feeling down, speak up.

So how do you hold on to yourself when you leave your career temporarily behind?

First, set goals for this time. You may not know how long you're going to be out of the workforce, so for now use the time wisely. Write down five key things you want to accomplish. We realize it's not like you're on vacation and sipping smoothies all day—running a household is all-consuming and leaves one with less free time than you might expect. About half of American women say they have no time for themselves. But what are the big-picture things that are important to you that you feel like you haven't had time to spend on? Maybe it's writing, learning a new language, exposing your kids to art, or visiting friends you haven't seen in a while. If necessary, find ways to do them with kids in tow.

Don't lose sight of what motivates you. Think about what appealed to you about your career in the first place and try to find that elsewhere, whether through volunteer opportunities or your community. When you can stay connected with who you were before having kids—what drove you, what made you the happiest and most proud of yourself—it can help you build the life you want no matter if you stay in the workforce or step back. Think about passions that died with your free time or the parts of your job you loved the most (mentoring others? data analysis?) and try to incorporate them into your life and protect the time as best you can.

Prioritize you. Like most new moms, when tennis star Serena Williams's daughter Alexis was born, Williams was completely wrapped up in her. She wasn't thinking about her game; she was grateful to be able to just be with her baby. But, according to the website The Undefeated, her trainer told her, "You're making time for everyone but yourself; just like they tell you on the airplane, you put your mask on first." Don't lose yourself. Let's take working out: it can feel like a huge time suck, between getting dressed for a class, getting to the studio, working out, getting home. Finding gyms or studios with child care is a great option, but so is running up and down the stairs. When Stacey couldn't get to the gym, she would run up and down her San Francisco hill ten times as her neighbors gave her the side-eye. I didn't care, Stacey says. I know I'm a happier, healthier, better mom when I exercise. And if that means enduring some odd glances, so be it. There are millions of Instagram accounts of moms doing push-ups while their kids are taking a bath. It can be hard to find the motivation to do that, but if it's important to you and if you're the type of person who really benefits from exercise endorphins, make it happen.

Outsource something. With the preposterous amount of mess children create on a daily basis, you can start to feel like your entire day is spent cleaning up and putting things away. And that weighs on you. This is a tricky topic: hiring help doesn't come free and many women are not comfortable with it or can't afford it. In a survey conducted by *Real Simple* and the Families and Work Institute, more than 45 percent of women said they would *not* hire more household help, even if they could afford it; and 69 percent say they would *not* hire extra child care if they could afford it. The reasons range from needing to be in control to martyr syndrome because it's their "job." Many women we talked to who leave work take on every house-related responsibility because they feel guilty that they're not contributing to the household income. They can't justify having cleaning people when they're not working. We need to break these patterns. If you're feeling overwhelmed by housework, talk to your partner about how you can adjust your budget. Sending your laundry to a dry cleaner can easily save you up to five hours a week. Or think about hiring a young mother's helper to watch the kids (on the cheap) so you can catch up around the house and maybe run an errand. Look at your household work like you would your job: What is best for you to take on yourself? What can you delegate? Also, give yourself a break—your home doesn't need to look magazine-cover worthy at all times. A little mess just means you have a well-lived life.

Find a squad, stat. Going from the structure of work to no structure and no adult conversation at home is too drastic without support and a village. Jen says the time she had to develop bonds with moms during her break was invaluable: My mom friends keep me sane. We look out for each other. They also are my go-to in an emergency, which I've already tapped many times since I went back to work full-time.

Prioritize social time. Take the time to search for resources that help stay-at-home moms connect with each other and that get you out of the house. There are local mom-focused Facebook groups (just search for one with your town name), libraries, the Y; churches have new mom groups, too. Or just strike up a conversation on the playground with someone you think you could relate to. It feels awkward, but once you open up, you will be pleasantly surprised by how many other parents are looking for the same thing. Finding other parents you click with can be hard. Remember, everyone is in the same boat, so start by putting yourself out there.

Own your story. Think about how you will answer the "What do you do?" question. It's a question that can be unsettling for some, especially when you aren't really sure what you want your future to be. Amanda Schumacher always had a high-profile career in media communications, but when she left her role at the *Huffington Post*, she didn't know what to say when people asked her what she was up to. "It was hard for me to not have a big, impressive career to talk about," she says. Amanda was happy with her decision to spend more time with her kids, but she struggled with her identity—even when she began consulting and freelancing after just a six-month break. Was she still a working parent? Stop worrying about making other people comfortable. Stacey's friend answered that she was on a ten-year career hiatus when she was probably just a few years into her break, which allowed her to own it. Some women write into Après that they're returning to work after a five-year "sabbatical." Avoid using the phrase, "I used to be . . . ." Say you are an X who is on a career break or moonlighting as a mom. For example, you could say you're a user experience lead who worked at start-ups and agencies and is on a two-year hiatus with your boys.

Feed your brain. Why are we constantly encouraging our children to try new activities and classes and be open to everything, but as adults we don't follow the same advice? When you're feeling like you have nothing to talk about but your kids, change that. You have the power to stay relevant. Many parents lament the lack of time to read books. We get it. But you have to make time for what you need to be you. Is there a night class you can take? Maybe you miss family dinner once a week to make it. Or can you listen to a daily podcast while you're driving all over town? Don't give up on intellectual stimulation. Classes, alumnae events, book clubs, and discussion groups all present opportunities to meet new people. If you can't find one, start one!

Prepare yourself for career FOMO. There will probably come a time when you hear of a former colleague, most likely someone junior to you, getting a big promotion. You will have that wave of doubt and question your decision to leave. And, you will look back on your workdays with rose-colored glasses—how glamorous they were! Expense account lunches! Traveling to interesting places! Brigitt, an editor, says, "When another friend of mine ultimately accepted the job I turned down, I felt a little sad and wondered if I made the right decision. But those feelings are fleeting and very minimal compared to the amount of times I've said, wow, thank goodness!" It's that perspective that helps.

Learn from men who stay at home. The National At-Home Dad Network says there are nearly 1.4 million dads taking on the role as primary caregiver. And while being a stay-at-home dad can bring forth a wealth of fresh challenges (fighting gender norms from the other side and trying to make mom friends at the playground without seeming like you're flirting, for one), there is one thing we can all learn from them: the ability to ask for what they need and not feel guilty about it. When stay-at-home-dad Ian's wife was pregnant with their third child, he wasn't afraid to tell her that he was going to need help. The two older kids were now in full-time preschool and Ian was looking forward to catching his breath a bit. They decided to find a part-time day care.

Learn to be present. It's easy to get caught up in the stress of parenting, especially if you're second-guessing your decision to leave your job, but there is tremendous value in taking a career break—for you and your family. View this time in your life as a reset opportunity. Be present. Stay active. Keep one foot in the door. Know that this time at home is temporary (if you want it to be) and therefore should be valued while you have it. Stacey's sister Carrice found herself being called by recruiters regularly while on her own career break and she learned to say, "I'm one year into a two-year break to be with my boys but would love to connect with you when I'm heading back to work. Thank you for reaching out to me!"

If the decision to leave the workforce was not totally in your control, do what you can to prepare yourself for when the time comes to get back to work. There is always something you can do to keep one toe in the water of the working world—keep in touch with colleagues, read about relevant topics in your field, or take an online class. The point is not to feel like a victim of your circumstances but to do everything in your power to set yourself up for future success.

Redefining Your Relationship

Most women we surveyed gushed over how supportive their partner was about her decision to quit. And, as we've said, it is much easier when one partner is home: fewer scheduling conflicts; an ease of anxiety that a family member is there for your children; perhaps even a delicious dinner on the table waiting for you when you get home. But let's not get ahead of ourselves.

When you're not in the workforce, it changes relationship dynamics and can put a real strain on your partnership. There can be an imbalance of power—and everything that comes with warped gender roles passed down from the 1950s. "Looking back it was a complete surrender to my husband," one woman confessed. "He then was not only one hundred percent responsible for us but I was one hundred percent financially dependent on him." It's enough to push a woman over the edge—and back to work. You need to talk about clear expectations for yourselves and each other before you make this decision: What will your partner still manage even if you quit your job? Is he on board with that? You need to set up expectations with your partner and feel like an equal even when you don't contribute financially. You need to make time for just the two of you. Here's how to avoid other common pitfalls:

Know you still have a voice. Just because there may be an imbalance in paychecks, it doesn't mean that one partner is not pulling his or her weight (unless they're not). We both have the most supportive, wonderful husbands who never made either of us directly feel less-than for not working or working less. But it really bothered me that I wasn't contributing to the family's finances, Jen says. It was probably in my own mind, but I felt like I didn't have enough of a say. It's natural to succumb to these feelings, but don't walk on eggshells. You are still a team and you are both supporting your family in your own way.

Keep your own bank account. Having access to your own money allows for financial freedom. We both did this, knowing there would be a point when we would want to spend money without discussing the purchase with our husbands. Talk about how the finances will flow when you leave your job. You're equal partners moving money around and no one's self-worth should be on the table. "The term *allowance* is rubbish, and a woman should never feel that she's asking for it when she has decided to stop working," says Sherry.

Divvy up responsibilities. Yes, the partner who is home will automatically take on more of the household responsibilities. But that doesn't mean your spouse should get off scot-free. That will only lead to resentment. Choose what each of you will own and don't look back. If he's got the cars and their maintenance, he's responsible for scheduling service appointments—and going to them even if it's during the day! Be realistic, be compromising, but don't take it all on yourself. You have made the decision to be your children's primary caregiver. That is a job. Running a household is a job that the whole family should contribute to. Including your kids. Studies have also shown that having kids do chores creates a stronger family unit and children are actually happier as a result.

Keep those lines of communication open. When you're feeling like you're being taken advantage of or not respected, or any of the million anxious conversations women tend to have in their minds, bring it up. Jen would think—gee, I complained when I was too stressed from working, and now I'm talking about being bored with not working. I'm going to drive my husband crazy! Well, maybe. But it is always best to talk it out. Remember, this is an extraordinarily transitional time in your life—lots of changes, lots of emotions—and it's okay to share those feelings with your significant other.

The Ideal Career Break

Taking a career break to be with your children or family—or for yourself—offers a chance to see what new gifts and talents want to come out and express themselves. It is like hitting the pause button to see what else feels interesting, alive, and challenging inside of you.

You're never too old for a second act. Nora Ephron was fifty-one when she directed her first movie. Nancy Meyers was forty-eight. Nancy Pelosi raised her five children before turning to politics.

When you start to look at your life through this lens of purpose (aka, what you would do if no one was watching or paying you?), you begin to see that you have been growing possibilities for your new career all the while you have been at home with the kids.

The truth is, there is no magic number or formula. Every woman's path is unique; every family is different; every career is different. It's wonderful to not have the stress of work and it's wonderful to only focus on your family and your home. But if you're used to a big career, it might get old quickly.

Here's what you *do* need to know: Finding a full-time job after a one- to two-year break is significantly easier than finding a job after a seven-year break. Many companies like Netflix, Etsy, Spotify, and most in the United Kingdom already offer paid family leave from six months to a year. Companies see a break of that length as "acceptable." If you take a one-year break you won't have to explain away a gap, and you'll still be close enough to your last day of full-time work and network that it's significantly easier to bounce back. And that's what more than 40 percent of Après members take—a brief break, just one or two years.

For financial reasons, others have an eye on kindergarten, meaning when their youngest is eligible and ready for full-time school. It also tends to coincide with the moment parents realize that while you can fill your day from 8:30 to 3 p.m. pretty easily, there might be something else that would be more satisfying and lucrative to spend your time on. Depending on the age range of your kids, this means a minimum of a five-year break.

That said, if you've already been out seven years or aren't ready to go back after one, don't panic. Yes, if we were to generalize, the length of your career break directly impacts the amount of time it takes to find a job—that is, the shorter the break, the faster it will be. But the real hidden variable is how work-ready you keep yourself while on a break. Say Suzy has been out five years; after she quit, she didn't keep in touch with any of her former colleagues and didn't keep any of her work skills fresh. Jane had been out for eight years but kept up with her colleagues, volunteered with purpose, and made a point to read up on industry trends. Who do you think is going to have an easier time getting a job? (Hint: It's Jane.) The most important meter is not always how long you're out, but how long it's been since you've been in touch with the gatekeepers of your career opportunities.

When you quit, set a plan of action. We know that many women just put blinders on and hope that everything works out in the end. Jen admits to this. I walked away from the stress and didn't think twice about how seven years of radio silence with all my former colleagues would impede my career comeback, she says. I thought, I have the skills, I have the experience, *of course* I will get a job again. It can take at least a year to find a job that you love. And while we know you *will* find your way, we want to better prepare you for the transition. Research shows that most women want to go back to work at some point; go into your career break with that mind-set.

There are a few things you should absolutely do while on a break. Keep those business networks going. Continue to do things that challenge you. Take a class. Stay engaged. Discover what you're truly passionate about. And write it all down. Because when the time comes to return to the workforce, you'll need all that information to get back in the game.

But you know that. We all know that. It's too easy to slip into a I'm-focusing-on-my-family-now mind-set and beat yourself up because you *haven't* responded to that text about drinks from your old coworkers. Just start somewhere. Taking a pause from the working world allows you to slowly build back your career path and keep that fire stoked. Here are the three things you should try to make time for:

Maintain your professional relationships. Today, when roughly 80 percent of jobs aren't publicly advertised, the "it's who you know" mantra rings louder than ever. And if you don't keep in touch with your former colleagues and contacts, that circle will get a lot smaller. Pick five to six quality network contacts and drop them an email every few months just to say hi or ask what they have going on at work. Make a point to see key members of your support circle at least once or twice a year. You know, the ones who would have your back, or advocate for you for a promotion, or be the first to let you know about a new opportunity. "I'm a really good networker," says DeNora Getachew, who works as the New York City executive director of Generation Citizen. "So even while I was home, I stayed connected with my network, I set up coffee dates to talk about what's going on in the workforce, so I knew where I would step in and where there were opportunities."

Don't let the world pass you by. Watch TED talks about the latest ideas while you're waiting on the car-pool line. Read current events to stay relevant. Stay up on the latest technology. Try new apps for your industry just for fun. Basically, don't let brain fog creep in for too long. "Life is long, careers are long, and the world keeps changing so much," media executive Bonnie Fuller said at the 2018 BlogHer conference. "When I was starting out I never thought newspapers and magazines would go away. There was no such thing as the internet. I realized that I was going to have to learn a whole new skill set. The ability to be open to change and learning more is essential." Stay fresh and be able to adapt.

Stay active on LinkedIn. Follow former colleagues if you hadn't previously. Respond to their posts to keep your name fresh. You should update your LinkedIn profile to be more representative and goal-focused of where you are right now (remember that elevator pitch?). Your bio gives you the best opportunity to say something like: "Media Account Executive looking to translate skills into freelance and consultant work focused on XYZ." Even if you don't actually want to be a consultant at this point in time, keep your bio fresh. Engage on LinkedIn: thumbs-up big news for people; share others' posts. You don't have to post yourself—just be an active listener. Let people know you may not be making your own news now, but you're happily watching and supporting those around you who are.

But most important, value the time. Know it's a piece of your overall career pie, and maybe a delicious slice.

HOW COMPANIES CAN SHINE:
Keep your alumni close.

Establish a commitment to women who decide to take a break by staying connected and even offering continuing education while they're on a break. Remember, 40 percent of Après members take just a one- to two-year break so the amount a company already invested in them is worth keeping the door cracked open. McKinsey & Company is well known for its revolving door of welcoming its former consultants back to work after career breaks. Here's how to do it, too:

1. **Make it easier for women to come and go from the workplace.** Follow PricewaterhouseCoopers' lead and mentor women while they're out. The PwC program allows a woman to leave the company for five years but stay connected and educated (she is paired with a "buddy" at work during her time out and the company pays for continuing education).

2. **Develop communication tools to stay in touch.** Start a company alumni group on Facebook or LinkedIn and use it as an opportunity to let former employees know about returnship opportunities, company news, and other ways to keep them

engaged and interested in the latest from the company. Provide memberships to women in leadership groups (check the Chamber of Commerce in your area and discover other local groups) for a set amount of time after they leave to keep those ties to the company.

3. **Host panels and workshops to spark dialogue.** Because Joanie Harrington left on a positive note, she is viewed as a role model and valuable resource to many former colleagues who continue to reach out about the best ways to stay, leave, and set themselves up for success. One woman told us, "I wish my company would have had a panel of other parents of young children talk about their experiences. It would have removed my doubt that I could be successful and be a new mother. I wouldn't have felt so alone." Create opportunities for people to come back and reengage with the workforce.

CHAPTER 5

THE CASE FOR FREELANCE, FLEXIBILITY, AND PART-TIME OPTIONS

Am I half in, half out?

It may feel like you only have one choice to make about your career: Are you all in or all out? The decision to stay or leave the workforce is not always clear. What if you could dial back the intensity? There is a wide spectrum of options, if you look for them—everything from freelance work to strategic volunteering; part-time to professional development.

It's worth it to look and see what's out there that could fit your needs. After talking to thousands of women about their return-to-work struggles—women from all different backgrounds and industries, in all phases of the Messy Middle—we know there is one thing above all that keeps a career alive: staying active and connected to your career in some way, shape, or form. This is not revolutionary advice. "Keep one foot in the door" is a common career adage. But what does keeping one foot in the door mean?

How can you actually do that and still be responsible for your kids during the day? What's the right ratio, or the right balance to make it all work?

First: imagine your career as a dial. In some years, that dial is going to go all the way up to 10, maybe even trying to push the limits beyond that. In others, you're going to turn it down *way* low. Just don't let it get to zero. To help with that, establish your primary career goal of the moment. This could change on a month-to-month or year-to-year basis. "I wish I had known that people move in and out of modes of work all the time—part-time, full-time, home, office—and I wish I would have had more confidence to try something short of quitting and see if I could make it work," says Margaret, who works in public policy. "But I felt guilty and thought I was letting my coworkers down by working from home or missing a staff meeting. Now I realize, I was really good at my job and they may have been happy to let me go freelance for a while." You can't know unless you ask or do the research.

A friend also on maternity leave tipped me off that our maternity leave paperwork allowed for a part-time schedule, Stacey says. But I had to make the ask. After Rory was born, I spent a lot of time thinking about how I could keep my place in the newsroom while spending more time with my daughter. After years of asking other people questions professionally and after years of asking for what I wanted at work—more pay, better assignments—I asked the hard question: What would it look like if I worked *less*? I asked to go part-time . . . and the *Wall Street Journal* agreed. I did it for two years. It allowed me to take Rory to music class on Thursdays and quell my personal guilt of leaving her with someone else for fifty-plus hours a week.

No one at the company suggested it as an option—there's often very little communication for parents about what the on-ramp back could look like post-baby. And there are misguided assumptions about what being a less-than-full-time worker means.

There's a perception that part-time or freelance jobs don't lead anywhere, and that the lack of pay isn't worth the stress of working. We don't agree and believe that repeating these perceptions causes people to look down on these schedules, for one, and two, puts women in a place of feeling stressed about decisions when it could be far simpler. Will you make less money working part-time? Likely. Can you get ahead of this by understanding that and working hard to protect those days you aren't working? Yes. Can you potentially make more money freelancing? Absolutely.

When you work part-time, you eliminate large gaps on your resume and keep your skills fresh. It also allows you to be creative with your time. Is this a good time to experiment with running something of your own or trying a new role? Could you pitch a job share? We've interviewed women who have "leveled down" in seniority in exchange for part-time, only to level back up when ready, and others who shifted to jobs that weren't exactly their area of interest but allowed them to keep working and have better work-life balance.

Maybe your goal is to just "not be obsolete" or "find part-time work in a year." Maybe your goal is to test the waters on consulting as an independent contractor. How much time can you devote to your career right now? Even if the answer is close to none, there are plenty of ways to stay fresh and keep your mojo alive. This chapter will walk you through the possibilities, paid and unpaid.

Strategic Volunteering

Volunteering at a place where you can see your children is a smart strategy for multitasking moms. However, the little secret of the

PTA, HSA, or whatever school organization you're a part of is that these jobs take *a lot* of time. We are not understating their importance—the women and men who step into these roles are positively impacting your child's educational experience. If you are going to carve out the time for a big job like president or volunteer coordinator (we're not talking about class mom or field trip chaperone), choose a role that suits your career aspirations and can translate to solid resume gold. For instance, saying I helped raise $100,000 for a school development fund is impactful. Being the webmaster or treasurer or sitting on a design committee for the twenty-first-century classroom can all translate to experience.

Karen Brewer, previously chief marketing officer for technology companies and now managing director of Brewcrew Consulting, says she got a little restless while scaling back her career and agreed to be the chairman of the steering committee to rebuild her town's park. "A few other mothers who had also left the full-time workforce joined me," says Karen. "We developed and executed a plan that included fund-raising, design, marketing, PR, and grant writing all with kids in tow." It was personally rewarding, she says, and also a great way to keep her business skills sharp, involve her children, and give back to the community.

Volunteering was also key for Julianne, a social services lawyer. When she took a career break, she began volunteering for a local nonprofit that helped troubled youths—a cause she was passionate about. After four years, that nonprofit asked Julianne to come on board and work as a part-time lawyer. It was an amazing opportunity for her to have a doable schedule, have a short commute, and work for an organization she really loves.

Volunteer work can also give you the gift of discovering new passions. Ellen was an art teacher for ten years, did some freelance assessments at various schools for another eight to ten years, and volunteered in the kids' schools and about town for sixteen years. Now Ellen works part-time for a design firm while she builds her own business. "My interests changed, or rather evolved and were rediscovered, while I was home volunteering," she says. Ask around for opportunities: be on a board, help a local small business—something that keeps your skills sharp or builds upon them.

Professional Development

If your industry or company values advanced degrees or earning extra professional development credits, going back to school is another smart move. Teachers can earn salary bumps for professional development, or having an MBA could put you in a new salary bracket. If you can squeeze it in now you may be saving yourself from challenges later. Jen took a few college classes during her break and loved the experience. It was great to get out of my regular setting and meet people who did not view me as a mom, she says. I was a student, just like them. Also, I enjoyed learning about a new subject and challenging myself academically. Of course it wasn't always easy to do "homework" during weekends, but ultimately the experience was one step toward helping me back into the workplace. Look for online classes for grad school (Carnegie Mellon and the University of North Carolina at Chapel Hill offer online MBA programs); maybe you can take one class a semester? Yes, it could take five to six years to complete your degree, but if you're planning on being out for that long, it's a win. We recognize that higher education comes with a hefty fee. Do the cost analysis—will you actually get a salary bump from this or will it make your return to work easier? Ask the program if it has placed grads in their forties or fifties. If so, look at this as an investment in your comeback career.

If you prefer the DIY education route, research what skills are most needed to stay fresh in your role. There are millions of YouTube videos, webinars, and classes for learning a myriad of skills. "I went to NYU, took an advanced course in a similar industry that was on the rise," a UX (user experience) designer told us. "There was a high risk in pursuing the new career, but there was more risk to try to stay in the same lane knowing that it wasn't going anywhere." Is there essential knowledge you must keep up on for certain fields? Developers will need to know the latest programming language trends, and doctors should keep reading medical journals. Keep going to professional meetings (even if you are transitioning industries) quarterly—maybe two from the industry you left and two in the industry you hope to go—to understand what you need to know.

Also, even if you're not sure you want to stick to the same career, do the minimum to not let your license lapse. Nurses, for instance, can simply take continuing education courses to keep up with their requirements. The regulations for lawyers vary state by state. In California you need to register every year with the state bar association (and pay the fee) and have continuing legal education credits (between twenty and thirty hours for every two years). If you can't find the time to do this, you can get your license back after it expires—you just may be subject to additional testing (and who wants to do that again?). Check your state board for your industry to find out the rules.

Freelance Work

Taking on freelance or consulting work is one option to keep your experience fresh and your foot in the door. By 2020, an Intuit study estimates that more than 40 percent of the American workforce, or 60 million people, will be independent workers—freelancers, contractors, and temporary employees. In fact, 31 percent of Après members are looking for project work because it allows them to earn money while prioritizing family.

Many people recognize the tax benefits of freelancing or working for themselves, and the ability to buy health care outside of an employer has made it possible for individuals to not feel "tied" to one company. It can give you incredible autonomy, and many people we talk to report making more money when striking out on their own.

Lorien Gallo had risen to the VP level at a very young age. She had a big job with global responsibility and traveled nonstop. And a ten-month-old. "I was burning out and I felt like I was missing out on my life," says Lorien. She decided to leave her full-time role, have a second and third child, and consult. She started her own consulting practice for the flexibility of picking and choosing the projects she wanted to take on. "Ideally in between nap times!" she says. "I would not trade that time for anything," says Lorien, who has since returned full-time as the VP of human resources for a medical company. "However, I am so grateful that I had the foresight to keep my foot in the door by consulting and keeping in touch with all of the executives I worked with. It helped me in the long run."

But not every industry translates directly to project-based work, and finding freelance work can be challenging. First, define your specialty: What are you an expert on? If there's something you know a lot about, embrace it. Even if it's Excel. There are companies looking for remote analysts, or organizations who need help bookkeeping. Are you an SEO whiz? Think about your top, most in-demand skills and search for those keywords at Après or LinkedIn. Create a profile on freelance marketplaces like Upwork. "When my son was born I needed to stick to set schedules and this limited opportunities," says Melinda, a former magazine editor. "I'm in a constant state of imagining what might be a fulfilling use of my skills and how I can convince someone of that." Melinda shifted her editorial skills to marketing opportunities because that was where the freelance market was thriving.

Spread the word that you're looking for work. Ask your former employers and colleagues—they know you and what you can deliver. Let your network know what kind of freelance projects you're looking for and have a place to direct them for more info, like a personal website. Even a simple one designed in Squarespace or Wix can show off your resume, recommendations, and portfolio of work. If you're in a less creative field, maximize your LinkedIn page with lists of clients and links to projects.

Once you find the work, now you have to figure out how to get it done. The hundreds of freelancers and consultants we spoke with all said the biggest challenge is feeling like you're straddling two worlds and never having enough time to do it all. To be the mom at pickup but also the one writing well into the night; or to take on a two-week project when your child-care coverage just simply isn't enough. Here's how to manage common mistakes they all made starting out.

Set a strict schedule. How many hours do you have to get the work done? Be realistic about it: Is it when the kids are at school? At night after they go to bed? Laura Vanderkam, author of *I Know How She Does It: How Successful Women Make the Most of Their Time*, found that nearly half of high-earning working parents regularly work after the kids go to bed. Know that this schedule can be hard to maintain. One woman told us her freelance schedule just wasn't sustainable. "I was working as a freelancer in the field I so loved from 7 p.m. until 2 or 3 a.m. (once the baby was asleep) and then waking up at 5:30 a.m. to nurse, etc. . . . I was so exhausted I knew I couldn't sustain that lifestyle."

Working from home, even when kids aren't around, can be a true test of procrastination and focus. Your eyes will glance over to that pile of bills calling your name; you go to make lunch only to realize there is no food in the house and you must go grocery shopping. Or you tell yourself a thousand excuses, like throwing a load of laundry in won't take too much time, right? Eliminate these distractions by reminding yourself you must work during this time. You are working. This isn't an exercise in fun. The dishes can wait. Distraction is the number one enemy of any freelancer. Especially one who is minding the fort. Social science shows us it can take twenty-three minutes to get back to the task at hand.

Block your time and internalize this mantra: when you're working you're working. Don't check social media; don't whip out the Instant Pot. Get out of the house, if you can. Create a realistic schedule (use your Google calendar or notebook) and write down everything you need to do. Schedule in things like driving to activities and making your own lunch—these things take up time and prevent you from getting your work done. You want to make sure you can do everything you've promised.

Compartmentalizing work from home tasks will help make your work better while also drawing the line in what others might expect you're able to accomplish (that is, all the laundry and cooking) just because you're home, and hopefully avoid any associated guilt. It's good advice if you're working full-time but remotely, too.

Figure out how much to charge. This is hard. As women, we tend to undervalue ourselves and our work. In the 1990s, researcher John Jost found that women paid themselves 18 percent less than the men paid themselves for identical work. Sadly, this has not changed. Linda Babcock, professor of economics at the H. John Heinz III School of Public Policy and Management of Carnegie Mellon and coauthor of *Women Don't Ask,* found that when women do negotiate, they ask for 30 percent less money than men do. To determine your value, first look to Glassdoor for standard market rates and ask other freelancers in your field who you are close with to open up and share. We're not naive; we know most people are funny about finances—"Almost half of Americans say that the most difficult topic to discuss with others is personal finance and they would rather discuss death, politics or religion," writes Kathleen Burns Kingsbury in her book *Breaking Money Silence.*

Fran Hauser, media exec, venture capitalist, and author of *The Myth of the Nice Girl,* says it took her a long time to ask people for compensation as an advisor. Fran loves to mentor others. She is passionate about it and would often offer entrepreneurs advice for free, but as the requests grew exponentially, she just couldn't handle the time and energy commitment. She decided to rethink how she responded and put parameters around her role as an advisor. She would do a thirty-minute introductory meeting for free, but after that she would ask for compensation as an official advisor. When she has casual networking meetings with other advisors, she asks them, what kind of equity do you ask for? It helps her stay on top of her market value.

Another simple formula: Think about what it will cost you to get the job done. How much will you have to pay in child care? Transportation? Those should be your baseline to break even. On top of that, add in a surcharge for your brainpower and emotional energy. You can also think back to your last salary and divide that by 2,000 (40 hours a week by 50 weeks—freelancers don't get paid vacation) to get an approximate hourly wage. What you start at might not be where you end.

Plan for the unexpected. What happens when a client needs something ASAP after 3 p.m.? Do you have backup care you can rely on? Whether it's a helpful friend or a drop-off activity place, make sure you have a network to help support you when you need to work when you least expect it.

Learn to pass on projects. Part of protecting your time is being selective about the new projects that will come your way. It's common to say yes to everything because you're nervous that freelance work will dry up or you will lose out on an important opportunity. But the worst thing you can do is overcommit and deliver mediocre work. Or, on the flip side, having your head buried in your phone 24/7 and losing out on that quality time with your kids (remember, that's why you went freelance in the first place!). Be clear with clients on when you can really deliver work, or deliver a firm "no." They will appreciate it, and it won't jeopardize future opportunities to come your way.

SIX WAYS TO TURN DOWN MORE WORK . . . NICELY

Is your workload bursting at the seams? The next time someone asks you to work on a project that you know you would love to help out with, but you really don't have the time for, try one of these comebacks to make you sound polite and professional—and keep getting more work.

1. "I am working on a number of projects until [insert date]. Afterward, I'm happy to discuss taking this on." Or "I could get this to you by [insert a date that's actually realistic]. Let me know if that works on your end." Only use this one if you

don't have the bandwidth to take on the assignment right now, but it sounds exciting enough that you'd want to work on it in the future.

2. "I wish I could help, but I know I couldn't give it the time it deserves right now." Use this if you really don't have a ton of interest in the project but want to keep the door open with the client. People appreciate honesty instead of delivering a subpar product.

3. "I know [insert name] is really eager to take on a new project—perhaps you could reach out to her?" Use this one if you really, actually do know of a star freelancer who is hungry to take on a new assignment, but needs a sponsor like you to mention his or her name. This will help you in the long run, too.

4. "Unfortunately I'm not taking on extra clients at this time, but I can recommend [insert person]." Similarly, this is a good response if you're a therapist, photographer, wedding planner, or any type of consultant. Recommending someone else equals sweet, sweet karma.

5. "Unfortunately I'm not taking on extra work at this time, but thank you for thinking of me!" This is a nice, succinct response if you're a freelancer with a very full plate.

6. "This sounds like a really exciting opportunity, but my schedule is full and so I'll have to pass at this time." Perfect for when someone wants you to attend an event or conference.

The trend here? Start with something positive—you wish you could help or it sounds like an exciting opportunity, and then turn it down without feeling like you need to offer much detail. You don't. You just need to say no—that way you *both* can move on.

Part-Time

Going part-time might give you the space you need to be who you are right now. Life and career coach Johanna Beyer tells us that taking a break—or in this case, working differently—can be good for your career. It gives you the space to potentially be even more creative. And there's no doubt you'll be more prioritized, efficient, and productive.

Thirty-four percent of Après members consider the ideal job to be part-time work that's less than twenty hours a week. It's not surprising. Pew research data found that 46 percent of married mothers who made "work sacrifices" with a reduced schedule were happy, whereas only 31 percent of full-time working moms could make the same claim.

Many women worry that going part-time will derail their career or that they will work a full schedule and be paid for only a percentage of it. Others worry they won't get benefits. Remember this: it doesn't have to be permanent.

Be assured there will be a future. I never thought part-time would be limiting, Stacey says. I looked at it as a necessary next phase. After I had my first baby, I was caught off guard about how long it took me to recover and heal. Five months later, I was ready to go back to work, but also felt a sense of sadness because I loved being with my daughter. I thought pitching a part-time schedule was a good way to test the waters and navigate my role without having to be full-time. I wanted to be around more for my daughter. I saw the value in that for me and for my husband. I decided on a three-day schedule, Monday, Wednesday, and Thursday, which allowed me to keep my benefits. It worked well. On Monday we would meet and plan for stories and use Wednesday and Thursday to execute on them. Eventually Rory had the same preschool schedule so we commuted together. In the end, I stayed for two years in the part-time role before launching my own business. I know firsthand that a switch to part-time does not mean your career will not progress.

If there are no part-time precedents at your company, it doesn't mean it's off the table. Bettina was running the research department at her company, a fast-growing start-up in San Francisco, when they asked her to take on the additional responsibility of managing the sales marketing team. Oh, and there wouldn't be a raise or title change. And she was pregnant. And it would mean even more travel from her base in New York. But she loved her work and really believed in the future of the company, so she agreed to it. While on maternity leave, Bettina knew she would come back to work. "I had been at the company since the very beginning and loved what we were building," she says. "That said, you start to run the numbers in your head for the cost of child care and you gain a newfound confidence and perspective of value." So when she returned, she had a plan. She was going to ask for a promotion with a salary increase, and if that was met with a no, she would propose an alternative part-time role that didn't require travel. She suggested a prorated salary decrease for the reduced hours, but increased stock options. They agreed to the latter. "I never would have had the guts to go in and ask for what I wanted, but after I had my daughter, my priorities became clearer and I gained a new level of confidence in being willing to do that. My world didn't revolve around my job and career anymore. When you have other priorities, it can give you a broader perspective." Shortly thereafter, the company stock took off and she ended up with a four-day workweek job that had a higher overall compensation level than any salary increase would have given her.

Some women worry about future career ramifications from scaling back to part-time. "It was scary to admit to my boss that I could not continue full-time, having worked so hard to reach certain goals and levels," says Jean, a health-care manager. "Knowing my group could not accommodate part-time at this level, and facing the distinct possibility of having to resign or accepting much lower-level work and pay to work part-time was terrifying." But it all worked out. Jean says she discussed her need to change and though they weren't able to staff her as part-time, they facilitated a meeting with another group that were desperate for good staff and were willing to try a new-to-them concept of part-time workers.

And, always, fight for what you need to make life work for you. "I am only twenty-five years old, so I definitely felt weird asking about a flexible schedule, but employers are shifting and are becoming more and more willing to be flexible in order to get great talent," says an Atlanta woman. Speak up and advocate for yourself, because no one else will.

Job shares are less common, but Morgan Tully is proof that they can work. She was a senior sales manager at Google for thirteen years before she had her first baby. Once she returned after maternity leave, "I wanted to duct-tape my baby to me, but I also wanted to keep working," she says. She worked with senior management to arrange the elusive job share, partnering with a woman on the opposite coast. She worked Monday, Tuesday, her partner worked Thursday, Friday, and they overlapped on Wednesday. "There were challenges, but you're getting two senior people, basically for the price of one—I don't understand why there's such a stigma that it won't work! It really is about having a manager who is open and receptive to the arrangement."

The hardest thing about working part-time is teaching everyone else—your boss, your colleagues—what it means that you work part-time. You have to constantly remind people of your workdays and will get eye rolls and then consider calling in because you could do it for ten minutes while the baby is napping. But stop yourself. There's a little joke about women working part-time—the woman agrees to work less and the employer agrees to pay less—and the employer always keeps its end of the bargain! You just have to do one thing to make the guilt go away: remind yourself, they're getting paid to work on Tuesday and you're simply not.

Look to the pharmacy industry—it's setting the bar for successful part-time work. Harvard economics professor Claudia Goldin found that pharmacists had the smallest gender earnings gap and the smallest penalty for reducing to part-time work. Why? Technology enables pharmacists to leave a comprehensive record of each client and provides access to information about the client's medical history. Because of this seamless exchange of information, the industry welcomes part-time work and doesn't penalize its employees for taking advantage of it.

Many women who follow a part-time path are anxious that they need to prove themselves as a valuable employee. When you *could* hop on a Friday conference call, but it's your day off and you *could* take the kids to the park, what do you do? There's no question being successful in a part-time role is a true art and a test of your time management prowess. But if you can survive the growing pains, it's a great option for women who have the opportunity to turn the dial down a bit but remain active employees.

It's important to note that part-time can be challenging for hourly workers who already make a low wage, and part-time often translates to unpredictable schedules, which is very difficult when you need to sort out child care. If you fall into this category, look to companies that will provide certainty in scheduling, and aim for ones that will also offer you benefits.

Flexible Jobs

With forward-thinking companies understanding the need for cultural workplace reform, now is the perfect time to pitch for a more accommodating schedule. There is no one definition to flexibility. It means different things to different people. It can simply be coming in earlier and leaving earlier; or working from home one day a week. It can mean full telecommuting or a compressed workweek (forty hours in four days).

With so many options available, first consider how your ideal week would unfold. Do you prefer to work from home one day a week or work only four days a week? Is it a shift in hours (coming in early, leaving early) or the ability to be home for dinner one day a week? And think about why you need or want flexibility. Maybe it's to avoid a long, unproductive commute. Maybe you really want to be able to drop your kids off at school once a week.

Think about the cadence of your work (are Mondays particularly busy?, are there all-hands meetings on other days?) and your family's particular habits (car-pool needs are out of control on Wednesdays) to figure out what's a good solution. Having a clear objective and the confidence to ask for what you want will ensure your ability to negotiate.

"I wish all employers, including my most recent past employer, would be more flexible with working parents, recognizing they often need to be in two places at once," says Lauren, a fund-raising manager. "And flexibility allows workers to get more done, too." We live in a modern age, with technology, so working remotely is a very good option to offer, support, and even encourage—it allows workers some flexibility that day with their children (pickup/drop-off) and even allows them time to get more done without the distractions of coworkers or the workplace.

Prepare to make the ask. Do your research before you approach your boss. Search for precedents at your company: Does anyone in the organization work from home? What's the arrangement? If you don't know, go to HR and ask for the policy. Then, predict what your boss's concerns might be, whether it's not being in person for a last-minute client meeting or that it will be harder for her to manage your time. Have a plan as to how you're going to address those issues.

Present flexibility as a win/win. Draft an opening script that says you want to work together to figure out a way to allow you to work from home. Don't come at it like, "Here's what I want and why." It should reflect that this is a problem-solving conversation. It is important to note that this arrangement should benefit both you and your company. Instead of viewing it as an accommodation, be sure to present the value to your employer. Why do you think this would be beneficial for the company? Companies don't say yes to be nice. They say yes to benefit the company.

Be flexible with how it could work. Maybe it's one day a week, two days a month; let your boss propose a date first. Remember, this is a negotiation so figure out what you really need and what you really want. The more options you present, the better your chances of finding the perfect fit. This can be a boon for your peers as well! If your boss is still hesitant, propose a trial. Say, let's try this for two months and regroup to talk about what did and didn't work.

Be a great flex worker. If you succeed in convincing your employer that you can effectively manage a flexible schedule, your job is to continue to be productive, communicative, and reliable in your new schedule. It may take a bit of trial and error to find the most effective way to work from home. It sounds a lot better than it actually is, being pulled into two worlds. Even with a flex schedule, the demands of motherhood are a part of your mental load. Finding balance at work and home is the dance that mothers will always perform. Show your company that it is possible to master or at least manage it.

As the desire and need for flex options rise, more companies are offering company-wide benefits. "We are seeing significant trends in the flex work realm," says Amy Elisa Jackson, editorial director at Glassdoor. "They have to attract and retain talent." According to Jackson, Dell, Aetna, Apple, Kaplan, and American Express all offer flexibility options and have benefits packages that note the kind of flex work that's possible, and companies are launching perks like "Work from Home Wednesdays."

Taking a career break—or dialing it up then down—won't kill your career. In fact, having these years of life perspective can make you a more valuable employee. There is magic in taking a break. We're going to help you use that to help you get back.

HOW COMPANIES CAN SHINE:
Be flexible.

Companies need to recognize that as the world has changed, so has the way we work. Before the internet, you *did* have to be at your desk for set periods of time so you could answer the phone and make decisions with your coworkers. Now technology can connect workers across the globe. But it goes beyond the tools; it's about creating a culture of trust.

1. **Be open to flexible and creative work arrangements.** Flexibility is not one size fits all. Flexibility advocate Werk has developed trademarked terms to describe modern flexible scenarios like DeskPlus: employees can work out of different offices if available; TimeShift: an unconventional schedule (that is, shifting hours, or breaking into two chunks). Other ideas: Try radical-candor calendaring: encourage execs and senior management to calendar personal things—a haircut or basketball pickup or yoga class. That sends a powerful message. Also, consider a formal or informal job-share scenario and set boundaries: No meetings after 5 p.m. unless critical (day cares close at six). In a tight labor market, flexibility can be a strong recruiting tool.

2. **Create an environment of trust.** If you offer flexible working, destigmatize it. Fitch Ratings, for example, proactively embraces agile work arrangements and highlights the people who are doing it well. "We think that it is key as an organization to embrace and encourage flexibility, for the women *and* men in our company," says Jamie Krulewitz, managing director and head of global talent for Fitch Ratings.

3. **Train managers on how to manage remote and flexible workers.** To be successful, companies must give people the tools to make these policies work and train people how to manage flexible and remote workers. And when there is someone who is a "bad flex worker" and is taking advantage of the policies, get HR involved to help manage that person. Don't let one bad apple penalize an entire workforce.

PART II

RECONNECTING WITH YOUR PROFESSIONAL SELF

How to Return to Work After a Career Break

CHAPTER 6

GETTING CLEAR ON WHAT YOU WANT TO DO SO YOU CAN GO DO IT

Want to know a secret? Taking a career break can provide an incredible chance to reinvent yourself and find work that makes you really happy. Of course, it might not feel that way right now—getting clear about what you want to do next can seem overwhelming. The good news is, you don't have to know *exactly* what you want from day one. Think back to what brought you to your former job in the first place. Maybe it was a good paycheck, or a sense that you were making a contribution to a larger goal. Those motivations may have changed since you left the workforce, and now is your chance to look again toward new opportunity with fresh eyes—eyes that have the gift of experience, time, and likely a deeper understanding of yourself and the world around you.

Trust that turning the career dial to spend time with your children has given you a new kind of freedom. The freedom to try something different, to switch industries, to go back to school, or maybe even get your old job back. Be inspired that you can now reinvent toward something meaningful or more lucrative—with the smarts of earlier experience combined with new desires. For Mikal Finkelstein, a New York City pediatrician, her get-back path was volunteerism + school. Volunteer work in Haiti while on a break made her realize she could make a bigger difference in the world, and when she was ready, she started a master's program in global public health at New York University.

Thirty-six percent of Après members say they're unsure if they want to return to the same field they left, and 70 percent of members come to us for help with identifying a new career path entirely. These women may not know the what or where, but they are ready to explore the possibilities to work again.

Rest assured you are not alone in career choice confusion. According to LinkedIn, nearly half of all professionals ages thirty-five to forty-four say they don't know if they should stay in the same job or try a new field. LinkedIn deems this large group Career Sleepwalkers—they feel like they're on a work treadmill going nowhere but don't know how to step off. Now, you can't say the same for Gen Z and younger millennials. That same study found that more than 80 percent of people under the age of twenty-four would consider switching careers and they're three times more likely to change jobs than baby boomers. Use them as your inspiration. It's okay to be green. It's okay to test out a new field.

For Kristin Mann, who worked in finance, it was a Lyme disease diagnosis that led her to classical Pilates (the only thing that seemed to help her symptoms). She was so impressed with the results, she started training and studying to be an instructor. She now runs her own studio with a waiting list of clients.

For Susan Levitt, it was a leap of faith in the start-up world. After a six-year break from the corporate scene, she decided to return to the financial industry but at a smaller firm that was willing to take a chance on her.

For us, it was seeing a need for and starting our own company.

Whether you're going from finance to fund-raising or music teacher to marketer, you will feel unsteady from time to time. Here's what helps: Talk about it. Find people who have made major career changes. Share your fears.

"When a woman is ready to do the exploration and figure out who she is right now, it is an incredible thing to witness," says career coach Johanna Beyer, who runs On Your Path Consulting. You don't have to have all the answers. It's okay to fail. "Many of my greatest lessons come from failing over success," says Jami Miskie, a marketing executive. "I've pivoted my career multiple times and wouldn't have ended up where I am now without making the changes I did." You don't need to find a job for life—just something that allows you to make some money while discovering your passions, that provides an opportunity for you to learn, and that is fulfilling.

So What Do You Want to Do?

"How can I search for a job when I don't even know what to look for?"

We get asked this question a lot. Don't assume your old role is necessarily the answer. A great exercise is to first think about the *how* of the work versus the *what*. How do you want to work? Laura Riordan, PhD, a career and life transitions coach, offers a series of questions to help you define the work you seek: What kind of job is going to fit with your current lifestyle? How much time do you want to devote to working? How far are you willing to commute? Are you more inspired working in a group of people or by yourself? By answering these questions you can begin to paint the picture of the types of jobs and companies that would make you happy.

Once you have a sense of your ideal work structure and what will be satisfying, you can focus on *what* kind of work you want to do. It's a chance to fall back on old skills or turn toward something new. Start paying attention to what really interests you. What news do you keep up with/turn to every morning? What conversations do you crave with friends? Where does your mind go while working out? What podcasts do you listen to? This is why maintaining your sense of self and protecting and nurturing your identity during your leave is so crucial. All of these can be subtle cues about target areas that you could drill into and extrapolate into areas of interest for work.

Coach Beyer recommends thinking about your entire life and the jobs or experiences that lit you on fire and what sucked your soul dry. One client of hers shared that her proudest moment was when she rallied her high school to sell ice cream. That clued Johanna in that she was a natural entrepreneur. Her aha moment was when she was seventeen but it stuck with her. "Nothing is silly from your past," she says. If you're stuck, think back to when you were a kid and you were asked, What do you want to be when you grow up? You always had a quick answer: a fireman, a chef, a police officer, a space warrior. Tap into your instincts; don't overthink it. As we say, just start trying things. You never know, princess-scientist does have a nice ring to it.

Next, turn your attention to the *why*. What are you hoping to gain from it: your career back? Work that keeps you busy? Something with more meaning? Most women we speak to want to do something that's interesting—they say, *I want a job that aligns with who I am and what I care about.* Our most popular workshop focuses on purpose and passion.

A career break can help your purpose come into crystal-clear focus. My ability to go part-time, while countless of my friends worked in industries that simply did not permit part-time schedules, made me realize that something had to change and that more women should have the ability to create their own career path, Stacey says. Why was I one of the lucky few? It shouldn't be about luck. That's why I decided to start a mission-based company that set out to help women find companies right for them. And to put some of the ownership of the process in their hands and shine a light on companies that offered these schedules.

About 60 percent of Après members cite purpose as a reason to get back to work, and the work revolution army agrees. More than 50 percent of millennials say they would take a pay cut to find work that matches their values, while 94 percent want to use their skills for a good cause. The Deloitte millennial survey of 2016 deemed them the "Purpose Driven" Generation because of this quest for higher good. Millennials are disrupting the traditional workplace norms for the better. But researchers are missing a huge segment of this "Purpose" population: women who are returning to work.

What do you really care about? Jennifer Chow Bevan, founder of Path Relaunch, a leadership and executive coaching company, proposes this additional self-assessment:

1. Describe your ideal day. If money weren't an issue, how would you spend your time?

2. What are you most passionate about? What brings you energy?
3. List five dream jobs you would love to do or try if there were no limitations on skills.
4. What would you describe as a "peak moment"—a time you felt inspired, invigorated, or successful—in your personal life? Describe the details—who were you with, what were you doing? What made it a peak moment?

But purpose is so much more than a buzzword and not just a hunt for work that is "meaningful." Purpose is also when you own and celebrate what you do naturally, says career coach Johanna Beyer. Purpose is your calling card; it's what you were meant to do in the world. What do your friends and colleagues turn to you for? What is the compliment or acknowledgment you hear most often about yourself? What made you feel accomplished or led to others recognizing your work? These are big clues of your key strengths and what you do well.

It can help to get an outside perspective: talk to people who know you well or with whom you've worked, including past colleagues, fellow board members, or executive directors of nonprofits for which you've volunteered. Ask them when they've seen you at your best. What were you doing when you stood out? How did they see you having an impact?

Look for themes that arise. "For example, one of the themes that was clear to me when I thought about these questions was that while my previous careers centered around critical thinking and problem solving, what I enjoyed most was the teamwork, camaraderie, and mentoring aspects of my roles," says Jennifer Chow Bevan. "In fact, in looking at past performance reviews, I saw a trend that most managers gave me kudos for my soft skills— relationship building and ability to understand people dynamics. Finding a new career where I could flex these skills to the max became my new focus, leading me to become a career coach, which has been the most rewarding—and fun—career I have had!"

Knowing what drives you + your core competencies = an effective job search.

Your strengths are what you're going to pitch to potential employers later. That's how you're going to sell yourself and tell your story.

Figuring out your purpose also gives you a big advantage: it's an amazing vetting opportunity. "Knowing your purpose allows you to look at jobs through a new lens," says Beyer. "It keeps you from being desperate and only saying yes to what is well aligned with you." That said, be patient with purpose. You're not always going to find a job that hits all the marks right out of the gate. You might have to take a job that brushes on your passion and your talents, but is low-paying/grunt/not exactly right work. It will come, trust us. One investment banker we know wanted to become a jewelry designer. She needed to gain experience to learn the customer and business sides of the business so she completely pivoted and took a retail sales job on the floor at Tiffany & Company. She thrived in the sales role for more than a year, and leveraged it into a bigger role. Don't count a job out because it's not what you want to do. Think of what it can lead to.

Maybe all that time volunteering in the school library has evoked a yearning to be a librarian? Or walking your dog and meeting other dog owners has made you realize that working with animals gives you a sense of fulfillment and you want to use your legal talents for the ASPCA? Purpose can lead you in a whole new direction—we say embrace it and see where it takes you.

Do You Need a Career Coach?

Hiring a coach can give you the kick start, motivation, clarity, or game plan you need to have a successful job hunt. Costs can vary from one hundred to several hundred dollars an hour. They can often see things that you can't. The trick is to find one that specializes in women who want to return to work, and ones that fit a niche that you need. What is your biggest pain point?

The coaches we have worked with have different specialties. Some are more tactical (how to craft the perfect resume); others are more life coaches, helping you answer the bigger questions of your values and motivation.

Then there are soul-searcher coaches who can help you find purpose and help you carve out your path back in. "I wish I had worked with a career coach and done this work to figure out what kind of work would make me happy and be family-friendly before our oldest daughter was born," says Julie, who left her job in financial services. "I always assumed that a career coach was a luxury that I couldn't afford and that I 'should' be able to figure it out on my own. When I was pregnant, I assumed I would go back to my old job full-time and just be somewhat stressed and unhappy, but that I would make it work somehow, since that's what everyone around me seemed to do. I had been unhappy in my job for years, but the birth of our daughter gave me the courage to finally make a change. I wish I had taken steps to find that courage earlier so that I wasn't juggling a newborn and a career change at the same time."

Christina Dahlberg agrees that a career coach was easily one of the best investments she ever made in herself and her future. While every arrangement is different, Christina, for example, spent one hour a week for ten weeks on a phone call with her coach. She says it was part counseling, part encouragement, part job search 101, and part accountability. "Working with a good coach is similar to therapy, because the entire job search or career change process is fraught with anxiety, insecurity, and lack of direction, even if you are a very confident person." Job searches and career changes take time and effort and very focused attention, which is where a highly skilled career coach can make all the difference.

When You Want to Return to Your Former Career

Some women do know that they want to step back into the same job or the same industry that they left. For these women, their first to-do is to look into how their industry has evolved, who is currently doing their old job, and where their former colleagues are working now. Though it's not necessarily easier to find a job, you have the benefit of focus. You know what the prize is, which will make the quest more efficient.

First, search for your most recent title on job listings to understand what kinds of jobs are being offered in your industry. This does two things: 1) informs you of what's going on in your industry and 2) gives you a gut check about how it feels when you're looking at these types of roles. Does it put you in a panic? Does it make you excited? When you go through the description, there may be parts of the job that you recall loving and you can later use those key words to see what new roles or fields there may be that focus on those skills. You want to learn what the basic responsibilities are and what they're being called (for example, maybe a digital marketing manager is now a digital analytics guru).

If you know you want to return to your old industry, hiring a career coach with insider knowledge will give you a leg up. We get asked all the time about job titles and what they mean and if what you were doing before the break even exists anymore. The truth is, if you worked at a marketing company, marketplace trends (and roles) can change in a year, while other fields like education or accounting are, on average, more straightforward to slide back into. Salaries change, too—a career coach will be able to help you set the bar. For example, in the legal world, salaries at large firms have increased significantly—a first-year associate now makes $180,000 a year, which raises the level for all other salaries.

Knowing what you want to do can be tactically easier (you may have contacts, you already know the biz), but it can also be more emotionally challenging (your colleagues may have all surpassed you by now) and humbling (this used to be really easy).

Regret is a word we never like to use, but when you know you want your old job back and there's a person doing it who seems half your age (or isn't doing it as well as you could have), thoughts of regret will bubble up. There's no way you don't consider an alternate reality—the one in which you didn't quit. Jen did. When I read in the paper that my former junior colleague was now running a baseball team, I nearly passed out from envy, she says. But then I have to remind myself of all the good I gained from taking a break. Like my son! We never would have had a third child if I kept working full-time. And when any self-doubt about my decision to leave creeps in, I know with absolute certainty that I would not change a thing.

You have to let regret go and focus on the future. Think of an amazing moment you had during your career break—either of a dear friendship you made, or the fact that you were there to help your kids through a difficult time, or that you could spend more time with an elderly parent or grandparent. These are precious moments that you would have missed. Let that power you forward.

The Truth About Switching Industries

We hear a lot of occupation regret. Women say if they had "known better" or "really thought about it" they wouldn't have chosen a certain career path that demanded long hours or wasn't accepting of family time. Peggy worked on Wall Street before having children. "After returning to work after having my first, due to my travel and husband's investment banking job, there was one period where my child didn't see either parent for five straight days," she says. That was the moment she knew one of them couldn't remain in the industry anymore. "If I had been really self-aware and chosen a different occupation from the start, I think I could have had the full-time career pre-kids and parlayed that into some part-time activities while raising them—perhaps as a marketing professional or accountant." This was twenty years ago, when there were very few remote/part-time alternatives in the financial services industry.

But before you subscribe to industry stereotypes or how "things used to be," know that times are changing. "Ten years ago it was very difficult to work in a flexible way in a law firm," says Kathryn Sollmann, author of *Ambition Redefined*. "If you said I want to work part-time or take a couple years off it would be the end of your quest for partner track. And now, so many of the big law firms are helping women continue to advance with more flexible schedules." Case in point: Jen and the firm Epstein Becker Green. The stereotypes of lawyers are that they work you to the bone, but Jen has found a firm that is open to a flexible schedule. Joanie Harrington, who worked at Barclays for more than three decades, agrees and says workplace conditions are slowly improving in the financial world, where in an attempt to retain women, companies are recognizing the need to offer flexible policies.

And just because you did one thing for fifteen years doesn't mean you can't move into something different. Industries that potentially didn't exist when you started out, like cyber security, financial technology, educational tech, all need talented people. And your skills may be more transferable than you think. A beauty executive told us that she had design experience in a certain niche and she wanted to use her talents in another industry. "My boss at the time made me feel like it would be impossible to make the change. I still remember he said something about 'Michael Jordan tried to play baseball, and that didn't work out.' What a jerk!" Don't let shortsighted people dissuade you from a let's-get-creative search. You don't have to start from the bottom if your role transfers to another industry seamlessly. For instance, a paralegal and her research skills would be great for a grant writer position. E-commerce sites need business minds; nonprofits need events people; start-ups need grown-ups.

Juanita Soranno had two young children and a job in finance that she didn't love, but she couldn't quit because her family relied on her health insurance (her husband is a personal chef). Instead of looking at this as a defeat, she thought about what did excite her. She loved her year spent teaching English in Korea, but didn't want to become a teacher in the United States. Instead, she came to the realization that she wanted to learn how to code. But before she committed to this pivot, she wanted to be sure this was really for her. Women Who Code was holding their first ever conference, so Juanita decided to attend and hear firsthand what this career would be really like. She was blown away. "There were women who had been in programming for years, women who were just coming out of boot camps, and women who were interested in trying it out," she says. "It was such a supportive, diverse, and wonderful community, I knew I wanted to be a part of this and that I could do this. I could see myself there."

After much research, Juanita found a part-time program at Rutgers that allowed her to get a certificate in Full Stack Web Development while keeping her job. After she finished the program, she got a job offer from one of her instructors who works at Trilogy Education, a company that brings digital skills programming to the world's leading universities. It married her love of education and her new skills as a coder. Dream. Come. True.

Look at what's out there. When you meet new people, ask a lot of questions about their job. After Jami Miskie quit her job at twenty-six, she started attending panels to hear people speak about different professions. She treated it like career day at your kid's school. When one of the panelists, a special events manager at Macy's, described her role, it was like a lightning bolt struck. "It was totally what I wanted to do and didn't even know jobs like this existed!" Jami says. As luck would have it, the woman was an alum from her college and connected Jami with someone in her department who was looking for an assistant in community relations. "I hadn't heard of this department either, which combined events with nonprofit partnerships. Volunteering was a passion of mine so I really wanted this job." If attending panels and conferences isn't logistically possible, most organizations upload videos of them online.

Look to your friends who have made the leap back. What are they doing? What has made them happy? What is working with their schedules and their desire to still stay connected to their kids' lives? Tara Briganti was a top TV media salesperson for more than sixteen years. She had a full-time babysitter, two kids, and a third on the way when she and her husband moved to the suburbs. Her oldest was six and she decided it was time for a break. Tara saw this as a chance to be home with the kids while she figured out her next move. Now her kids are twelve, nine, and six and she just got her real estate license. Her friends encouraged her to explore the field because of Tara's negotiation and business skills. For Tara, it also checked off many of the boxes for what she was looking for: flexibility, proximity to home, and the chance to try something new and different while utilizing past experience. According to the National Association of Realtors, for more than 82 percent of their members, real estate is a second or third career. Here's why they're drawn to it: 1) flexible hours, 2) a new interest in real estate (which might be a rite of passage for all "grown-ups,") and 3) a renewed entrepreneurial spirit.

Think about this: Something has changed since you left the workforce: *you*. And your responsibilities. And priorities. And maybe your passions, too. It's challenging to be a working parent so try to find a fulfilling career/company/boss/mission that makes it easier and worth the effort!

Alternate Paths Back

Going Back to School

After fourteen years of being an independent consultant, Megan, who had been a director of a software and consulting business, decided to study organization development and behavior. It was her consulting work that created a desire to further study how businesses are run, and she's about to start her master's program. To make a major career change, you might need to go to graduate school. For some roles, embarking on that career requires a new degree or certification (teacher, librarian, psychologist, accountant). But going back to school can also help you explore new fields to help you discover what you want to do. It's an expensive exercise, with the average school master's program starting at $30,000 and upwards of $100,000 or more for private schools, so before you apply, consider these points.

1. Can you do a trial period? Can you audit a class to see if you enjoy being in an academic environment again before applying to a full program? Or take classes at a local community college (less expensive and less of a commitment) to see if you genuinely enjoy the new subject matter.
2. Do they have success stories for older students? Has that program placed grads in their forties and fifties?
3. Do you have time to devote to a rigorous program? One word: *homework*.
4. Is there an online course or program that may be more accessible than traditional higher education institutions? Online courses don't equate to an easy Skype class. You still have a ton of work, assignments, feedback, and instruction—you can just do it on your own schedule.
5. Look at continuing education programs, too. You will get a certificate (not a degree) but it might be all you need to prove you have the skills to get the job. Just like Juanita!

Christina Dahlberg came out of the alternative-dispute-resolution field wanting to make a switch into social media marketing. But she knew nothing about it! So she paid $120 to take an online course, which required about ten hours per week of her time for six weeks. "It was worth every penny, and then some!" says Christina, who became a social media marketer.

Industries change in as little as two years. Even more "stable" professions like teaching and nursing have new curriculum standards, new hospital procedures, and new technology they've introduced. This can feel overwhelming, but if there is a learning curve, address it piece by piece. What can you do now to start educating yourself? When you break it down into steps, it feels much more manageable.

The Rise of Returnships

The concept of a returnship (return plus internship)—a program that offers a chance for smart, work-savvy, experienced women who left the workforce for an extended period of time to "get back in"—has been around for nearly a decade. In 2008, Goldman Sachs trademarked the term, and other companies, many in the financial industry, like Fitch Ratings, Morgan Stanley, Barclays, and MasterCard, also offer similar programs. But even hospitals, nonprofits, insurance, and tech companies are following suit, like the Cedars-Sinai Medical Center Physician Reentry Program in Los Angeles, which helps reinstate physicians who took an extended absence from practice. PricewaterhouseCoopers notes that 28 percent of global employers have adopted a formal returnship program to attract and provide opportunities for career returners. By formalizing and opening the door to smart women who want to get back to work, they are eliminating the "employment gap" discussion, which in itself is a huge confidence boost.

Returnships are a great opportunity to learn a new role, see if you like the environment and the industry, and prove your chops. If you are a great returner—work hard, get along well with others, show real potential—chances are you will be on a hot list for a job if and when one opens up.

Jenna Bloomgarden worked in equity research before she took a thirteen-year career break. She credits her returnship as the push she needed to get back to work. "It's easy to look at job descriptions and say, I'm not qualified for that . . . or that . . . or that," says Jenna. "It can really kill your confidence." Once she heard about returnships, she knew that might be the key to her start. Since she had worked on Wall Street, she knew she had the right credentials for the Morgan Stanley program, but she had been out for so long she didn't know if that was going to hurt her chances. "With a returnship, you don't have to hide what you're doing for your time off. They provide a great structure to get back in, and I feel like this was the best way for me to get back into this industry."

These get-back-to-work internships vary in length and style (the model at Fitch Ratings, for example, is a three-week intensive skills boot camp followed by a six-week rotation through various departments and then a final wrap-up week) and most of these programs are highly competitive (accepting only a handful of women, from about five to fifteen per year.) There is also a lot of pressure once you're in. "You're basically on a twelve-week job interview," says Jenna. "You need to impress your current boss, while networking and looking for opportunities in other departments." Jenna was fortunate to receive a placement afterward, but you're not guaranteed one. She recalls that there weren't openings for about a quarter of her class. But returnships can do more than direct placements. They provide an instant new network of like-minded, equally motivated women seeking new jobs—and access to an employer who is willing to hire them.

Jamie Krulewitz, managing director and global head of talent at Fitch Ratings, shares some insights on what their CreditPath program is looking for, but this can translate to most: 1) lateral skills or subject matter match, meaning a financial industry will want to see some sort of related financial experience, 2) professional communication skills: how do you carry yourself and communicate? and 3) critical thinking skills. During the Fitch interview process, they conduct a mini low-pressure case study where they ask the candidates to answer a question about a relevant scenario-based case. It doesn't matter if you know nothing about the subject matter; they are trying to deduce how you think about and address a problem (and if you're ready to do so in a high-pressure work environment).

Because these programs often aren't large and there still aren't a lot of companies that offer them in a structured manner, you might consider identifying a company that you want to work for and pitching the concept. Does the company you are interested in have full-time jobs describing something you would like to do but worry you may not be qualified for? Pitch them on a modified version that allows you to get some experience.

Starting Your Own Business

This one seems interesting, attractive, and daunting all at once, but between the rise of personal service businesses, Etsy shops, and everything in between and above, female entrepreneurship is a big business. In this country, women own 12.3 million businesses—40 percent overall, according to the 2018 State of Women-Owned Businesses, commissioned by American Express. The report also estimates that women are starting about 1,821 new U.S. businesses per day, a significant uptick from an average of 952 between 2012 and 2017.

I knew that running my own business would be a much bigger commitment than my part-time role, but I was driven by a mission, Stacey says. I often tell people I should have had my head checked for leaving a job and starting my own website! While I love the creative aspect and the autonomy, there are plenty of things I don't love that I still have to handle. Do you like sales? Do you like people management? I also couldn't have done it without an amazing legal partner and patient family (my husband in particular). Starting a business is not for the faint of heart and can be very lonely. If you know you like to be around people, don't start a business that isolates you. If you enjoy making every decision and holding all the responsibility, it's a career for you!

After a fourteen-year career as a photo editor for magazines like *Cigar Aficionado* and *Ladies' Home Journal*, Laura D'Abate embarked on a new role: owner of Pip n Bits, a custom bakery of cakes and cookies. Here's what she thinks you should consider before turning your hobby/hustle into a full-time gig:

1. Do you have or are you willing to devote the majority of your time to your hobby/hustle?
2. Do you have some sort of plan as to how you are going to market yourself? Can you start a website?
3. Are you able to problem solve on your own?

"I'm all for asking people for help, but problems will arise, and it is very important to be able to solve and work through these problems yourself. No one cares more about your business than you," says Laura. "Starting Pip n Bits was the scariest and most satisfying thing I've ever done," says Laura. "I have no regrets about turning my hobby into my full-time job. I've never worked this hard in my life, and never thought I'd work this much and not mind it. I'm tired and on my feet for fifteen hours a day, and still wouldn't change a thing." Many returners feel that if they're going to be working, it better be worth it. For many, starting their own business is.

To start, focus on an income-generating project—not just a hobby. "Remember the main benefit is extra income, not just a part-time job," says Chris Guillebeau, author of *Side Hustle: From Idea to Income in 27 Days*. Here are some other quick tips to know if you have the makings of a good idea.

Solve a problem no one else can see. Alli Webb, founder of DryBar, knew her friends wanted fast, easy blowouts so she created a business around that. As moms, Shannon Seip and Kelly Parthen were disappointed by the lack of healthy, kid-friendly options at local amusement parks and zoos. They launched Bean Sprouts Café, which provides just that.

Talk to your target audience about your idea. First, ask friends, family, even strangers about the idea. Then talk to the people most likely to use your service or product. Is there a clear group of people who would love this? What is their reaction to your idea? That will help you know if you have something there. And really listen. A very common mistake first-time entrepreneurs make is believing in their idea, even when no one else seems to like the idea.

Launch before you're ready. You need to know quickly if there's something here or not, says Guillebeau. Then regroup and see if your expectations were met. Was there a clear group of people interested in your product or service and willing to pay for it? If so, you might have something there.

Don't spend a lot of money up front. There are so many inexpensive tools to build a website or test a product idea. There's no need to pump a lot of money into an idea until you really know it has legs.

Women start companies, women start new careers, women change the world, women earn good money (or nearly 77 percent of what we deserve). It's really gratifying to do all that. Whether you're dying to get back to your old job or you've always wanted to make a career change, now's your time to make it happen.

HOW COMPANIES CAN SHINE:
Open the door to your company.

The quest for talent is an ongoing challenge for companies. There's a dearth of qualified employees in tech, for instance, and the competition for talent has likely never been higher. If companies created opportunities to access this highly educated, highly experienced talent pool—and test and train them—it would ease the transition back to work.

After analyzing their gender distribution, Fitch Ratings realized that the pipeline was leaking women at the director level. "As women progress in their careers and take on more managerial responsibilities, it tends to coincide with the inflection point of having children and weighing what to do next," says Jamie Krulewitz, managing director and global head of talent at Fitch Ratings. The company's CreditPath program is bringing back women at this level exactly where there was a need for diverse talent. The training program allows the organization to feel confident in their hiring decisions because they've been able to evaluate potential full-time employees in a more robust manner. It's paid off. The first year Fitch Ratings launched the program, they made six offers out of eight candidates. Here's what you can do:

1. **Provide a meaningful info session.** Host a Lunch & Learn session and invite women returning to the workforce. Provide a panel discussion with HR and business leaders that gives some insight into the company and why it's a great place (for women) to work. Give returners a tour of the office. Discuss potential opportunities at the company and if you have strong benefits and policies, flaunt them!

2. **Offer returnships:** We talk a lot about returnships in this chapter: the fact is they're a great way for companies to reach out to this cohort of women; give them the skills they need to accelerate their path back; and make the company look great in the process. Follow the lead of some amazing companies that are offering return-to-work programs for people who have taken career breaks: Goldman Sachs, MetLife, PepsiCo, Fitch Ratings, and Morgan Stanley, to name just a few. Access is one of the biggest challenges for this demographic and returnships provide that channel back—but they should be *part* of your recruiting strategy, not the only prong.

3. **Step outside your conference comfort zone.** Go where women are actively listening and talking about work and making it all work. Have your company participate in one of the hugely successful Conference for Women series that take place around the United States. For example, the Pennsylvania Conference for Women has more than twelve thousand attendees with household-name keynote speakers. These events are wonderful opportunities for your company to engage in an environment with thousands of women and discuss a hot topic of the day. Sponsor a panel and have your female employees talk about what it's really like to work at the company; showcase the wide breadth of roles and opportunities available to inspire attendees to consider a new career.

CHAPTER 7

THE HABITS OF CONFIDENT RETURNEES

Taking a career break helps you become more than you ever knew possible. You have the opportunity to reenter the workforce with so much more knowledge, perspective, and patience—kids will do that for you. It isn't going to be easy, but it's also going to change you for the better. It is going to make you even more capable than you could have ever imagined. You're going to discover energy you never knew existed, and that's inspiring and infectious to everyone around you.

You will also realize that your second act is a chance to do everything you wish you could have done the first time around but never seemed to find the time, foresight, or guts to do: to mentor others, to be more productive, to launch important programs and initiatives, to stop sweating the small stuff, to do work you really love.

The first time around, when my kids were young and I was still working, I always felt defensive and that I had to prove something to everyone: my boss, my team, my kids, my friends, Jen says. Once I was ready to return to work, those feelings were gone. I know

I'm a better employee because of my career break. Being a mother instilled in me a renewed ambition and sense of calmness—and an understanding and trust that everything would work out, even on those really tough days, because I always had something important at home that kept me grounded. Maybe it's being a little older and wiser, but I came back fresh and eager to take on the world.

We're not naive: you will still need to juggle. In 2014, nearly 75 percent of mothers with children between the ages of six and seventeen were working or actively looking for work, so you most likely still have kids at home under the age of eighteen who have needs. You will still need to make compromises and sacrifices. But the combination of work experience and fresh perspective that a career break offers makes you a stronger, more thoughtful, more willing-to-ask-for-what-you-want employee. Your challenge is to keep this confidence up so others can feel your back-to-work mojo (and hire you!).

In this section, we are going to get down to the business of exactly what you need to do to get a job and what you need to embrace on your comeback: overcoming your fear of rejection, taking steps to discover what you really want to do, learning to talk about your gap, and understanding how the job market has changed. Here's what else you need: a healthy dose of risk + knowledge of what's out there combined with the ability to problem solve.

Know the struggle is real. The Center for Economic Development reports "that having children *increases* men's likelihood of labor force participation while *decreasing* women's likelihood, even among the college-educated. Thus, among this population, the difficulties associated with reentering the labor force following a career break affect women disproportionately."

Sexism, ageism—they both come into play here. And we don't need data to tell us this; we know this through stories like Stephanie Won's. Won applied to *many* jobs on her return to work and found it was a tough process. "I went through countless interviews, and was rejected—and felt dejected—each and every time," she says. "When I felt burned out, I did pro bono work for causes I believed in, exercised daily, listened to TED Talks, and surrounded myself with people who believed in me and supported me."

Don't despair. We know it can be done with commitment and perseverance—drawing on your sense of self and leaning into the process. We know through countless stories what it takes and how to get you there. You will need to dig deep and get ready for the ride.

You *will* doubt yourself, your ability, your judgment, everything. The longer you've been out, the worse it's likely to be. But know that you're not alone and this scary self-doubt is temporary. Remember that trusted sense of self? This is an excellent time to bring that person to the forefront. Think back to when you were a fresh-eyed grad and first started your career—you didn't know anything, either. You probably weren't even sure if you wanted the job you got. But you took it day by day until you gained confidence and discovered what really moved and motivated you. Channel those feelings again.

Take thirty minutes to sit down and really remember all that you did in your career before your break. Write it down and let it sink in. *This* is the person a company will be hiring. Someone with previous experience. Bring *that* person to your return efforts. If you need to, post that list somewhere visible so you can keep the accomplishments you own fresh in your mind. In rediscovering your professional self, you will begin to remember all the qualities that you have to offer a company. Companies will only view you as a mother without work experience if that is how you view yourself. It is time to peel back the layers and recognize yourself for all of your talents, not just the talents that make you a great parent.

When you approach the job search with positivity, your network will take notice. Projecting the image of someone who has a renewed excitement about returning to the workforce makes you someone people want to hire. The world is changing and organizations are changing the stigma around taking a career break. There are employers out there who are willing to give you a shot, if you're willing to take it. Embody these best habits of returners to get into the right mind-set.

"Career gaps have become far more common in recent years— it's all in how you talk about it," Molly Saint, a recruiting marketer, told us. "It's really no different than preparing to talk about a previous job. Treating it the same way normalizes it, which I think is important."

Habit #1: Persist: This is probably the most important habit. Returning to the workforce *will* test your perseverance. It *will* test your confidence. The key is to never ever give up. Stephanie Won was a stay-at-home mom for ten years when her husband got laid off.

They had two kids under the age of ten, and two parents with zero jobs and zero income. Stephanie approached her job search with gusto and applied and interviewed with 29 non-profits, 37 for-profits, and connected with 50 recruiters before getting the offer she wanted. Phew. "The real win is who I've become in this process. I'm forever changed for the better— stronger, determined and proud," she says. Persistence and perseverance are essential.

Habit #2: Be patient: Once you decide to go back you may feel like you're behind already. Give yourself plenty of time to endure and enjoy the process. Unless you need to go back to work immediately for financial reasons, start your search at least six months before you expect to go back to work, knowing that it can take months, even more than a year, to find a job let alone the perfect job (one report says to expect it to take one month for every $10,000 in salary you're looking for). The best returners carefully contemplate their options and their alignment with their goals and family life.

Habit #3: Value your worth. Your confidence will take a hit; try to keep this at bay. Look at the time you took to be with your family as time well spent—one chapter that leads you to the next. Show how secure you are in your career decisions and no one will doubt them. This is invaluable. Alice Walker famously said, "The most common way people give up their own power is thinking they don't have any."

Habit #4: Ask for help. Confident returners understand that the professional world is a lesson in karma: what you put in, you get back. But sometimes, depending on where you are in the career continuum, you will be receiving more than giving. And that's okay. Especially if you are grateful and appreciative.

Habit #5: Don't be afraid to fail. Be open-minded, curious, and engaged in every conversation. Confident returners explore all avenues because you never know what door may open. Sometimes it will be the right one; sometimes it won't. But welcoming a chance to learn something new and to step outside your comfort zone will always lead you forward.

Making the Decision to Return

You don't wake up, decide you want to go back to work, and send out a resume that day. Your comeback starts with questions like "Is it time?" "Should I go back to work?" "What do I want to do with my life?" "What am I even good at anymore?" "Why do I want to go back?" For women whose youngest children have started full-time school and for those who find themselves empty-nesters or nearing that time in life, they often ask, "How am I going to fill all this free time now that the kids are gone?"

Nearly every woman we know who left a full-time job has asked herself one of these questions at some point. In fact, nearly 90 percent of women who leave the workforce want to return: Here's why:

1. Financial needs/independence
2. More free time/lessening child-care needs
3. Unexpected life events (divorce, etc.—see no. 1)
4. To be a role model for your children
5. Personal validation and ambition

Number five is so relatable, Jen says. I felt like I owed it to myself. I spent most of my life fighting for my education and my career, and going back to work would make all those years of school and working my way up the legal ladder worth it. I loathed the idea of dropping ninety thousand dollars on a law school education and never using it again. It seemed like such a waste. A few years after leaving Major League Baseball, I also began to feel that something was missing in my life. I quickly realized that the fundamental void was my career. Being a full-time mom was amazing and satisfying in so many ways, but it was not enough. I knew I was ready to go back when the number of existential crises I endured during car pool surpassed the joy I felt in having the luxury of time to drive my kids around. I needed to have work in my life that made me feel fulfilled. It took me a long time to come to terms with that, but once I did, there was no looking back.

Many women don't have the luxury of choice. It's an unforeseen life event that pushes them back to work: divorce, death, a partner's job loss, or other financial need. Take Erin Pruitt: She left advertising when her son was two because of travel demands. Ten years later, after she had had two more kids, Erin's husband unexpectedly passed away at the age of forty-seven. Figuring out what to do next was a long exercise in trial and error. She quickly realized after talking to former colleagues that the youth-worshipping ad agency culture was not the best fit for her return. She began to try jobs that matched her skill set (organization and project management) and her lifestyle (single mom with three kids), until she found what worked—part-time event management at a nonprofit, travel planning, and a career in real estate.

Michelle, a former retail international bond trader, found herself in the middle of a divorce after leaving the financial industry twenty years ago, before the recession and before she had kids. She took advantage of a period of layoffs and negotiated a package to make a change in her life. "I wanted to get pregnant, and I believe the high-stress level of my job was a factor in the difficulty I had," she says. "I just walked away; I had no sense of how long I was going to be out. I just wanted to have a baby." Now Michelle has four children and is getting divorced. "It's thrown me for a loop," she says. "After getting divorced, you look around and are like, what do I do now?" But Michelle says she's really enjoying the fact that her kids see her a little differently. Before interviews, they're saying, "Good luck, Mom. You'll do great!" And she's bonding over making resumes with her daughter who's in college. "Showing them that I can do this, that I can make it all work, is more inspiring than any 'you can do it' speech I could give."

Sometimes you do need a little push (and perspective) from your own family. Nancy Pelosi was a car-pool-driving, bake-sale mom who decided to run for Congress when she was forty-six. The daughter of a local politician, Pelosi interned for a Maryland senator before she began her family. She continued to volunteer for Democratic election campaigns while she was raising her five children. Staying home was important to Pelosi. She told *Politico*, "It is really an opportunity that you just can't get back, and you don't want to have any regrets about that." But when four of her children had left home and gone to college, Pelosi, who had an abundance of free time on her hands, considered an opportunity to enter politics full-time.

In that interview with *Politico*, Pelosi says she approached her daughter, Alexandra, a senior in high school at the time, with "a heavy dose of mommy guilt." She said, "Alexandra, Mommy has this chance to run for Congress, but it would be better if it were a year from now when you're in college. ... It's up to you, if you want me to be home with you, that's perfect for me." To which Alexandra replied, "Mother, get a life." So Pelosi started her next chapter. In 2018 she won her eighteenth election to Congress, at the age of seventy-eight. (Whatever your politics, you have to give a nod to Pelosi. She took a twenty-year career break and now holds the title of the most powerful woman in U.S. politics, ever.)

Silencing Your Inner Critics

Year one post-quitting was awesome, Jen says. I was enjoying my kids, loving life. Year two things started getting a little more real. I began questioning my decision, but I still didn't consider going back to work. Year three, I became antsy and started talking to a former colleague about coming back to the firm.

> **Jen:** Maybe I'll come back part-time.
> **Colleague:** We'd love you back three days a week.
> **Jen:** I would only want to come back two days a week.
> **Colleague:** You can't come back two days a week, Jen. Two days a week is not really working.
> **Jen:** All right, I'm not ready.

There's a fine line between fear and a subconscious lack of desire to work again—or a nagging feeling that you "should" work again. Especially when your youngest child is entering full-time school and you will have six kid-free hours on your hands (barring the inevitable sick days).

Figuring out where you fall is an exercise in self-reflection. If your brain instantly comes up with twenty reasons why it won't work out, you need to determine: Is that fear talking or an innate desire to not start the return-to-work process at this moment? It is most likely fear, Après coach Johanna Beyer says, especially if this sounds too familiar:

You're your worst critic: Your inner voice becomes louder and more rude. You ping-pong back and forth between two ideas, and your inner critic kicks in and tells you that both are bad options, which puts you back to square one.

You rationalize the abnormal: You start to rationalize that feeling underwhelmed, uninspired, and bored is just part of life.

You keep procrastinating: You set arbitrary timelines to procrastinate putting your dream into motion with thoughts like "I'll wait another year and then I'll make the change."

If you find yourself falling into one of these traps, you need to do a little more soul-searching. What are the roadblocks you see in front of you? Write them down, keep reading this book (!), and start addressing them one by one. Child care? How will you get a job? What do you want to do? What will you regret if you don't try? What do you need to get into the right mind-set?

Johanna says you will know you're really open to change in your life when you are actively questioning your current situation; when you're constantly looking at what everyone else is doing and thinking "their path is amazing!" Or when your internal dialogue gets stronger and whispers, "My children can't be my only purpose." In *The Feminine Mystique*, Betty Friedan wrote, "As she made the beds, shopped for groceries, ate peanut butter sandwiches with her children . . . she was afraid to ask even of herself the silent question: Is this all?" Most mothers we know have asked themselves that at least once (raises hands). There's no question the demands of motherhood have changed even since Friedan wrote her tome in 1963. Just watch *The Marvelous Mrs. Maisel*: mothers in the 1950s practically let kids raise themselves!

There are positive signs, too: You're craving the energy of the workplace and putting your brain to use. You're ready to start your own path back. And you have hope! You recognize that your excitement is greater than your resistance, and you take the first step.

In fact, taking the first step, however small, is key—finding a job again isn't always easy. If you've been out of the workforce it could take six months to one year of grit to find the right role for you. Of course it might happen faster than you were expecting!—just ask Jessica, a director of marketing. "I wish I hadn't been so afraid that I'd never be hired again," she says. "After I took a three-year break, I was hired again quickly and I maintained my level and salary!"

And while you should just start somewhere, you will be in a much better position if you are mentally committed to finding a job again.

Après members describe the decision to go back to work as overwhelming, confusing, and demoralizing. We've heard it all: Women stay in their roles because they're afraid they'll never be able to get another job; women avoid responding to work inquiries because they're scared their skills are obsolete. There's the fear of the unknown. The fear of being too old. The fear of spreadsheets. But you can't let fear hold you back from starting your next chapter.

Fear actually isn't always a bad thing, says Dr. Emily Cavell, a licensed clinical psychologist based in Los Angeles. "These feelings are healthy, and to be expected, when trying to make changes," she says. "The idea is to allow for the feelings of fear and doubt, while also taking steps to move toward your goals." From a lack of confidence to explaining a career gap, here are the most "significant concerns" and common fears for women wanting to return to work that we've heard.

1. I don't have confidence.
2. I don't have the updated skills required in my industry.

3. I don't know how to start my search.
4. I don't know how to represent my gap on my resume.
5. I don't know what I'm qualified to do now.
6. I don't know what skills I have that are transferable to the jobs I want next.
7. I'm worried about being an older person in a younger workforce.
8. I'm concerned about how my family will adapt to the change.
9. I don't know how I'll manage my time and have time for myself.
10. I am concerned about being rejected from jobs.
11. I don't know how to build my personal brand and online profiles.
12. I am worried that I am too behind in technology.
13. I don't have a strong professional network.
14. I want flexibility to be there for my kids.
15. I don't know what salary to ask for.
16. I don't think employers will respect the skills I have learned while caregiving.
17. How do I navigate passion versus practicality and money?

How many of these did you nod your head to? Number one is a biggie. All of this eats at your confidence in getting out there and applying. Statistics show that women won't apply to jobs unless they're 100 percent qualified (this means they can do every bullet point listed on a job listing). Have you ever looked at most job listings? It would be impossible to say you met every requirement, in most cases. Job descriptions are antiquated and have changed very little. Men of course apply if they feel they meet 60 percent of the requirements. Combine this with any lack of confidence in direction, ability, and commitment, and it's a quick downward spiral.

Wanted: A Confidence Reboot

A 2013 British study found that women on maternity leave begin to lose confidence in their ability to return to the working world just eleven months after giving birth (keep in mind the average maternity leave in the United Kingdom is one year). The report said: "Experts found millions of new mums cope admirably with the dramatic change in focus that comes with caring for a new arrival. But around the 11-month mark they are struck by a confidence crisis sparked by the feeling they are no longer capable of cutting it in the professional world. Fifty-seven percent say they no longer have the confidence or feel capable enough to re-join the industry and take up the same level of responsibility as before they had children."

You may be confident in your decision to go back to work, but that doesn't mean you have confidence. Being scared of putting yourself out there and looking for a new job is completely normal. "When we are out of the workforce, our measures of success are different, and we don't receive performance reviews, bonuses, or raises that help remind us of our value," says Barri Waltcher, a certified professional resume writer and the cofounder of Mind Your Own Business Moms.

Sadly, we're not surprised. For me, one of the most difficult points in my life was when I was out of the workforce and trying to figure out what to do, Jen says. When I quit, I wasn't panicked or nervous about eventually getting back in because I assumed that with my network and my experience as an attorney, doors would open again. It took a lot of elbow grease to pry those doors open and days of self-doubt, but all it took was one yes to put me on track.

Here are tricks for a quick confidence boost.

Go back and revisit your successes. Reflect on two or three times in your professional life when you accomplished something you are proud of. If you haven't already, start a get-back-to-work journal—write the stories down and notice the elements they have in common. Is it strong organizational skills? The ability to collaborate well with your coworkers? Interpersonal skills that create loyalty with clients? These are your strengths. You brought those qualities to your work in the past, you use them in your everyday life, and you will continue to bring them to your career in the future. There are qualities you have when you start your career that will grow with you and help you navigate no matter what happens. Remembering your strengths will help the process of rebuilding your confidence.

Remember you are experienced. Unlike someone just out of college, you have work and life experience that allows you to hit the ground running faster than others. Doubt will come, but do everything you can to remind yourself of your potential.

If you have children, put yourself in their shoes. Imagine if your son or daughter came home from school with negative thoughts or a lack of self-confidence. What would you say to them? You would remind them of their strengths. You would encourage them to be positive. And you would expect them to keep trying, even if failure was a possibility.

Elana D'Arciprete's daughters were two and ten when she separated from her husband. She quickly realized that she would not be able to support them on a teacher's salary alone. Elana said she could bartend or work at a hotel to earn extra income, but, instead, she decided to apply for a job at an insurance company, even though she had zero experience and no insurance license. "In my mind, there was little chance I would be considered. Still, something made me change the buttons on my only suit and wear hose and heels and show up for the interview. After a very brief meeting, I was offered the job and I signed the contract that day. Still not sure what made me sign it, but so thankful I did," says Elana. Now she's a managing general agent.

Take a risk. Risk taking builds courage. For some, it may be speaking in public. For others, it's applying for a job. And for others, it's launching a business. But the root of building confidence is to challenge yourself and take on whatever may be risky for you. While I was figuring out my next steps, I started training to be a Flywheel cycling instructor, Jen says. It was on my "bucket list" of things I wanted to do and I thought it would be fun. What I didn't realize is that teaching forty-five-minute classes in front of fifty people multiple times a week was like public speaking boot camp. It was a totally unexpected bonus.

Tell a friend. There is a definite snowball effect to admitting that you're thinking of going back to work. Research has shown that having an accountability partner, someone with whom you share your goals, can increase your chances of meeting those goals. It's this positive peer pressure that keeps you on track. Interestingly enough, it's also why couples who have a high number of attendees at their wedding tend to have longer marriages than those who elope—they don't want to disappoint their two hundred guests.

Just start doing things. Small steps, baby steps even, are essential to becoming confident—and confidence begets confidence. Good things happen when you are out and about. Nothing good happens when you're sitting at home in your pajamas feeling like you don't know what to do next.

Every day, try something new to get you pumped up to go back to work: Put together your killer interview outfit, ask a former colleague to coffee, ask a savvy friend for advice, start writing articles to post on LinkedIn.

Don't question yourself. In *The Confidence Code*, Katty Kay and Claire Shipman discuss the habit of upspeak—when you raise the pitch of your voice at the end of a sentence so it seems like you're asking a question, not making a statement. This subtly undermines your audience's confidence in you. Listen to what you're saying and how you're saying it—you might not even realize that you're doing it. Speak with confidence and others will listen.

It's not until you reenter the work world that you realize that everyone is fighting the same self-doubt fight. We remember being incredibly nervous for a meeting with Sallie Krawcheck's Ellevate. We had the typical self-deprecating thoughts, "Oh, they're so established. They know what they're doing. We're just this small start-up trying to figure it out." But you know what? When we got there and sat down in a standard office chair in a typical conference room in a normal office building, we realized they're just a group of people working really hard and sitting in a room doing the same stuff that we are. It was like taking the curtain off the Wizard of Oz.

With time and experience we know it's okay to admit that we have a lot to learn. There is a power, a gravitas even, from having the strength to say "I don't know" in a meeting. We've both reached the point in our lives where we're less concerned with people knowing we don't have all the answers. There's so much going on in the world, it's not possible to know everything about anything. It's much more important to know what people are saying than pretending that you already knew *CTA* is digital marketing jargon for Click-Through Action and not the Committee for Tired Attorneys.

Why Mothers Make the Best Workers

Here's what else should give you a confidence boost: Women returning to work bring forth an undeniable skill set. First, they're highly motivated. They're excited to dig back in and start putting their great work experience to use again. Second, they bring a fresh perspective—they have the benefit of an automatic big-picture view and don't get bogged down by inconsequential noise. Third, they're more productive. Alissa Quart writes about the Motherhood Advantage in her book *Squeezed*: "A cache of my friends and interview subjects told me that their work improved after their maternity. They reported that fundamental workplace skills like listening, reasoning, leadership, and scheduling had enhanced their labor rather than detracted from it. They even learned management skills from taming their toddlers. And a number told me they used their working hours better than they had before they had children, with improved concentration. A Federal Reserve Bank of St. Louis survey found that mothers were more productive in their jobs than women without children, a discovery obtained by surveying 10,000 academics."

Fourth, they make great role models and are more willing to give back. A very common complaint from junior women is that they don't have true role models in the workplace. Yes, are there senior-level women who seem to have no life outside of work? Of course. But most women don't want that to be their life. Returners are fantastic role models and a statement that the company is committed to women, even after they have children.

Overcome Your Fear of Rejection

If you've been out of the workforce for more than five years and didn't keep your foot in the door, it will take time to get you closer to the right job offer. We think it's best to go into every career phase with your eyes wide open. If you know what to expect, the good *and* the bad, it can help prevent these challenges from thwarting your motivation and prevent a career break from killing your career. Knowing what lies ahead can turn you into a warrior—not a worrier.

1. Less Pay and Fewer Opportunities.

   The bad: Studies found that opt-out women came back to jobs that paid, on average, 16 percent less than those they had before. The openings for senior-level positions are slim and the competition is high. Most employers, when trying to fill a position at that level, look to an internal promotion or someone, frankly, who is a safe bet without a career gap. Thus women often have to take a step back.

   The good: That step back can be temporary. If you prove yourself quickly—and the value that you bring to the table— you will find yourself with an abundance of responsibility. Any boss who realizes the talent they have on his or her team will want to maximize that. That's what happened to Ellen, a former art teacher who transitioned to an interior design career and a consignment liaison for Sotheby's Home. "What surprised even me was being hired quickly and recognized/ appreciated for the knowledge base and skills that I wasn't even really sure I had," she says.

2. Less Respect.

   The bad: Though a career break isn't an anomaly—and frankly, half of the male executives we speak to admit that their own wives have done so—there is still an unconscious bias against women with a resume gap.

The good: Companies are working to fix this by launching internal PR campaigns about the success of returnships and agile work policies. High-profile success stories help change cultural perception—like the recently deceased Brenda Barnes, who stepped down as president of Pepsi to focus on her family, then bounced back to become CEO of Sara Lee. Or Meredith Vieira. Or Serena Williams. Or Michelle Obama. Or any of the thousands of women we spoke to who took a career break and are now senior directors again. Once you break through the door again, that label of a woman who took a career break will be long forgotten once you are fully assimilated into the team.

3. Age Bias

    The bad: It exists. AARP says two-thirds of adults between the ages of forty and seventy-four have experienced age discrimination. Allison, a former lawyer, says it's been an uphill battle to find a job again, she believes because of ageism. "Unfortunately, I believe other reasons I get overlooked by employers is because they think I would get bored in the position because it's not a legal position or that because I have been out of the workforce for so long, I don't have the requisite skills," she says. She stresses that it's not true.

    The good: The good news about being a little older is that you have some pretty incredible life experience. Also, think of Jane Fonda, Ruth Bader Ginsburg, and Vivienne Westwood. We will assume that these dynamos have many years on you, and look at their continued success.

4. Rejection.

    The bad: The average rejection rate for any job searcher is extremely high (on average more than 100 people apply for any given job); for women who have taken a break, according to our coaches, it's even higher. Stay-at-home moms are half as likely to get a job interview as moms who got laid off.

The good: There isn't a creative genius on the planet who hasn't received a rejection letter at some point—Tim Burton, Madonna, Sylvia Plath, and U2 all have had the privilege. Rejection can motivate you to try harder; it can push you to refocus and explore a new, unexpected path.

In reality, there *are* a lot of job opportunities out there. In October 2018, LinkedIn reported 15 million active job listings. It might not be the perfect job, but it's one that gets you out of your house, gets you a paycheck, and might even offer some company perks.

Remember your motivation in getting back to work: more income, a stronger sense of fulfillment, the ability to contribute to society. Your time is now—go for it. It's about taking action now; it's about finding the mojo to hit the pavement; it's about seeking a network of women who are motivating each other to do it. We're not trying to get too hokey on you, but studies prove that a positive mind-set is your best asset to getting what you want.

We also want you to pause and think about the bigger picture of what it actually means for you to opt back in. While it is about you, it's also about so much more. Former Federal Reserve chairperson Janet Yellen noted in a speech that bringing more women into the workforce by making it easier for women to work with flexible work options, affordable child care, and better parental leave policies could lift the gross domestic product (GDP) by 5 percent.

And when you make money, you have money to spend, to save for retirement, and to donate to causes you feel passionate about—to put your money toward helping others. You also have the opportunity to help craft the workplace for other women. To make it better. To model the value of work to your children. You can't do that sitting at home.

HOW COMPANIES CAN SHINE:
Welcome back returnees.

Employers should recognize the value of women who are ready, willing, and eager to return to work, motivated and refreshed from their time away. Think of the value of hiring someone with previous professional experience who can slide into mid- to senior-level roles given their past work experience (which also happens to be where most companies struggle with gender diversity). Make it easier for them to find you. Here's how:

1. **Hold career events for people who have taken career breaks.** Visa, for example, offers a one-day workshop for returners covering networking and resume building; it's also a way to "casually" interview potential job candidates. Events like this can reduce anxiety for women contemplating a return to work, give them that confidence boost so desperately needed, and create a solid reputation for your company for overlooking the career gap. Other idea: host a session for back-to-work parents at "take your kids to work" day.

2. **Actively recruit this cohort of women.** Partner with organizations like Après to promote your interest in hiring from this demographic. Après member Maria found a job at K2 Intelligence on our platform after almost seven years on sabbatical leave being a mom. "This was a job that not only made sense to me because of my academic and professional

background, it was a job at a company that didn't see my absence from the workplace as a flaw, but instead chose to look at my strengths," she says.

3. **Shorten job listings.** Make them less intimidating. Yes, we know you're trying to weed people out, but a laundry list of requirements and arbitrary essential skills can also prohibit talented women from applying. Also, use apps that scrub out sexist language.

CHAPTER 8

TELLING YOUR (GAP) STORY

We are going to cut to the chase: don't apologize for your gap and don't try to hide it. When you're asked about what you have been doing since your last full-time job, answer the question and move on. One of the biggest stumbling blocks women make is not knowing how to talk about themselves and what they have been doing during a break. They worry hiring managers won't even look at their resumes because of it. They obsess over it and are convinced that employers will not value the time women have spent with kids or caregiving for others.

Women tell us all the time they can't get past the resume and the "black hole" of their gap. Jen had her own doubts and questions, too: What would I even put on my resume? Do I send in a resume to the HR vortex? Remember you have done so much good stuff—own it, don't apologize for it. We believe deeply that these caregiving years should be viewed as an asset and that it's time for employers to Mind the Mother Gap.

Gearing up for a job search is intimidating and exhausting—whether you've taken a career break or not. You need to mentally prepare yourself for the dance of job interviews, coffee date small talk, cold emails, follow-ups, and more. This can be fun, yes! You never know where conversations will lead you. But it can also be draining. You might even shake your fists for quitting in the first place. But you will find your groove. And you will get a job again.

The key is to nail your gap story. It's your returner's pitch. It's the answers to all those pesky questions curious contacts and hiring managers will inevitably ask you: What have you been doing "while not working"? "What are you looking to do—and why?" "Why now?" "Are you sure you want to go back? How do you know?" These questions can stop anyone in their tracks. Don't let them. Prepare your answers ahead of time and be authentic and positive in how you respond. Your gap is like the elephant in the room—it's not going to go away until you address it, but once you do, poof. It is easy for an interviewer to get over a gap if you show them how you're so much more than a time lapse on a resume; that you have a wealth of knowledge, talent, skills, and good-old gusto; that you're really interested in them and what their company is doing; and that you have a solid get-back-to-work pitch.

Being able to tell a good story is a talent. There's that adage, people don't always remember what you said, but they remember how you made them feel. It's good advice. When you begin a job search you're going to have to tell your story to everyone you meet, from moms at school and old colleagues to recruiters and interviewers, and you want to leave a memorable impression. Here are the steps to building, telling, and sharing your story with anyone who is listening.

Owning Your Gap

Step 1: Craft your gap story and practice your elevator pitch.
Stacey was on a call with a large sales company last year, pitching

the business, and the woman kept saying, "I can't believe we as a company have not tapped into this talent pool!" It was easy to convince her of the value of women who have taken a break. Keep that in mind as you begin to tell your story. A strong return-to-work pitch is composed of the past (why a gap) + the now (what excites you and why work again) + the future (what you bring to the table).

Own your gap and be confident with your answers. Be honest and succinct. You can even cut the tension with some humor. Jen likes to say, "I took a career break to raise some human beings," and always gets a laugh. Don't be sarcastic or self-deprecating, but showing that a gap is no big deal to you will convince others of the same thing. You should say whatever you feel comfortable saying—it could be that you took a few years off to care for your children and now you're ready to come back, or whatever your specific reason was if it wasn't about children. "People come to the table too defensive," says Cari Sommer, owner of Raise Communications, who left the legal world to start her own communications business. "Employers want to know what you can do for them right now. They don't care about what you were doing a year ago." Again, don't be defensive about your gap; talk about it.

Focus on the positive aspects of the gap. Talk about what excites you about returning to work. Your story, tone of voice, and energy should reflect your enthusiasm for reentering the workforce. Really think about your answer to this question: What excites you about working again? Authenticity will be obvious. When answering, "Why is now a good time?" don't focus too much on your personal details—you can simply say your children now have full-time care and you're eager to get back to the work that you love. Talk about how your career break allowed you to fully appreciate and value the work that you were doing or are planning to do.

Take inventory of your skills and expertise. Employers want to know how you can help them solve their biggest problems or grow their business right now. If you were responsible for award-winning ad campaigns at your last job, how can you show them you've still got the magic touch? Think back to the work to identify your strengths. What are you most proud of or what were your biggest professional accomplishments during your break? Did you take on volunteer work, freelance projects, or other relevant activities? You'd be surprised at how many people hit the pavement without even knowing what strengths they're trying to market. If you don't make it clear to prospective employers, they will not waste a minute of time trying to figure this out. One thing to be wary of: while it's true, convincing an employer that managing three kids' activity schedules has made you a project management whiz is a risk, depending on your audience.

Get right to the point. How can you describe your career and break highlights succinctly? Debra Wheatman, president of Careers Done Write, warns that this is not a time to "rattle off your life's story, go bullet by bullet over the points listed on your resume, or recite your certifications, degrees, and other qualifications." Instead, give some thought to what it is you want the listener to know about you. Your elevator pitch should boil down the most important facts about how you add value. Career coach Carroll Welch offers this example: *I am a former consumer goods marketing manager, and after taking a four-year hiatus to raise my children, I am looking to return to work in marketing with a health and wellness-related company. I've always been recognized for my focus on quality and productivity. My two years of experience with an entrepreneurial health-care venture have also enabled me to understand and anticipate what consumers want.*

Practice it! Speak it aloud in front of a mirror, then practice it over and over in as many kinds of real-life scenarios as possible. When you're at a coffee date, on the soccer sidelines, or at any event, try it out on people. Gauge the reactions and tweak your pitch as necessary. While your pitch will in essence remain standard, the level of detail and formality may vary depending upon whether you're meeting someone at a picnic or at a professional conference. You will want to tailor your elevator pitch to your audience. The pitch we give to corporate partners is different from the elevator pitch we would use to describe Après to a member. The one you give to a hiring manager will be different than to someone you are contacting for an introduction or just to share when they ask what you do.

If you want to improve your storytelling skills, consider taking a creative writing class. You'll learn the elements of a good story and most in-person classes require you to read your story aloud, which is great public speaking practice. You can even search YouTube for some great "perfecting your elevator pitch" tutorials.

Step 2: Refresh your resume.

Dusting off your resume is another difficult step for many women. It's one thing to talk about your gap and your strengths and accomplishments, but how do you synthesize that on one sheet of paper? How do you handle the gap on your resume? All these questions can feel paralyzing, and women tell us they feel like they have nothing to contribute to make their resume feel fresh. Changing that mind-set is your most important task. Your skills and talents have not evaporated—they just need to be brushed off and reframed for what you are now seeking.

A resume is more than just a list of information. It's a branding document that reflects your goals, your strengths, and your accomplishments. On average, hiring managers take ten seconds to review a resume before deciding to take you to the next step, says resume coach Barri Waltcher. You need to make a quick, strong impression, but don't let this info overwhelm you. It's the culmination of your efforts—your networking, your cover letter—that put together your entire hire-me package.

First, think about what you want your resume to say. If this piece of paper could talk, what is the perception you would want the recruiter to be left with? That you're revenue-driven? That you're a terrific manager? A big-ideas person? That you want to translate your finance skills into a fund-raising path? Go into editing and writing mode with that in mind. Think back to your elevator pitch—what phrases can you use to highlight your top skills and values? You want to keep the bullet points under every job simple and emphasize results, not responsibilities. Most activities ("raised funds") can be reframed as achievements ("raised $200k, exceeding fund-raising goals by 25%"), says Waltcher.

Your resume is an exercise in creative writing. Make a list of everything you've done while on your break besides taking care of your children, such as volunteer work, classes you've taken, or even favors you've done for friends. Stacey sits on a board that oversees a preschool in her neighborhood with a budget of $2 million and staff of twenty-five. The board recently ran an executive search to hire a new head of school, and she was part of the small team that led the search and hiring—this was real work that took a lot of time. How can you detail the volunteer work you've done to show financial or organizational impact?

Career coach and resume expert Jessica Warta has a client who loves data and analytics and had created a competitive pricing model for her neighbor who owns several vacation properties to maximize her rental income. On the resume, Jessica had her client create a role called Independent Financial Consultant, where she mentioned work like this and other pro bono services she offered friends and family.

Unpaid consulting work and volunteer roles should be grouped under one "Volunteer and Project Work" or "Independent Consultant" heading toward the end of your resume (note: paid consulting and freelance work would go at the top of your resume). List the organization name or type of work, what you did, and the results. Grouping it together tells the story of how you've stayed engaged and kept your skills fresh since your last full-time job. And do include dates. It's better for there to be a gap in dates than to write "CEO of Household" or "CEO of Jones Family, Inc."

Jessica says that most of her returning clients seem to discount major accomplishments because they think they were just a hobby or a passion project. Almost everything you've done on your break matters. She had one client who got certified and started a holistic nutrition consulting practice just for fun. The woman, who was looking to get back into finance, didn't think that was applicable for her resume. But it is! It shows drive, passion, and the ability to be a self-starter.

You can use those experiences to write your professional summary story, but the jury is out on including these summaries on resumes. Many hiring managers we speak to say that this formulaic bio can limit you and that they actually glaze over this jargon-laden paragraph. Others stress that for women returning to work, an objective at the top can give you the chance to summarize who you are and what you bring to the table, and reinforce your intent to get back to work. Jessica Warta has her clients write the sentence, "Seeking to reenter [fill in industry] in a role that capitalizes on my skills such as XYZ." Our take: write it and use elements of it in a cover letter but don't include it on the actual resume. Save it for your LinkedIn profile, where there's more room for the summary and it is frankly more valuable. It's best to customize your resume for each application to highlight your specific strengths and experience that match the role, so an overarching bio can be limiting.

Whether or not you ultimately decide to include this on your resume, having a concise, well-written paragraph detailing who you are, what you've been up to, and how you are the perfect person for the job is well worth the effort. You will need a professional bio or light cover letter in various forms during your job hunt: for online application systems, and for every email you send to a hiring manager. It's also a good opportunity for those looking to pivot to briefly tell their story. A lawyer transitioning into the nonprofit world, for example, should reference her pro bono work in her professional summary.

If this exercise is difficult for you, consider hiring a professional resume writer. They know the questions to ask and how to probe deeper to pull out important bullet points that to you might seem unnecessary. This might cost a few hundred dollars but it is totally worth it if it brings your resume into the modern world, helps you emphasize your skills, and ultimately lands you a job.

Finally, in your contact information, don't use an unprofessional email address. If you still have an AOL or Hotmail account, that will date you immediately. Sign up for Gmail now. Or, if your email address is too family-focused like bensmom@ or thejonesfamily@ you could jeopardize your chances, too.

Some more quick but essential formatting tips:

- Ask a friend in your industry to send you a redacted resume of someone they recently hired so you can see the most current and preferred format.
- Find someone to review whatever you write. Everyone needs an editor.

- Avoid ALL CAPS. Think modern, clean, and simple.
- Pick a clear font (that is, Times New Roman, Calibri) at a legible font size (no less than 10.5, depending on the font).
- One page is great, but if it looks cluttered, there is no problem with having a two-pager.
- Delete the antiquated line "references available upon request." (Note: you should start to line up those references before an interview.)
- Save as a plain-text PDF so electronic systems can read it.

If you find yourself tempted to go the Elle Woods route and print your resume on pink, scented paper, phone a friend instead.

Step 3: Get active on LinkedIn.

Don't underestimate the power of LinkedIn. It's your opportunity to inject the personality that your resume doesn't have room for and establish your own personal brand. LinkedIn has become *the* social platform to grow business connections, share your expertise, and get recruited. It's essential—whether you like it or not—to have a presence on the platform.

When Jen started Après, she did not even have a LinkedIn profile. Yes, zero followers, zero connections. But quickly, and we mean quickly, she became a super user. She did not do a mass connection request (note: even if it seems simple, do not fall into the LinkedIn prompt trap of instantly inviting all your contacts to connect with you—it's impersonal and can backfire) but she made a point to create a really strong profile (coaches can help with this, too) and began to strategically reach out to colleagues and connections.

Creating an engaging profile may seem daunting but once you have your resume done, updating your LinkedIn profile will be much easier, but still give yourself an abundance of time to work on the project (at least a week). And know these essentials:

Upload a professional profile photo. Use a nice-looking head shot—not a candid or photo of you with anyone else (this is the number one mistake people make). Use a simple background and make sure you look friendly and approachable—not too serious but not too smiley. You can hire a photographer to get this right for you, or ask a friend or family member to take a photo of you against a plain background. LinkedIn reports that members with photos receive 21 times more profile views and 9 times more connection requests.

Write an attention-grabbing headline. This is the first thing people see after your name that summarizes who you are and what you're looking for. You have up to 120 characters, or about twenty-five words, to put your intentions forth. Not a lot of room, which can honestly be a blessing. What is the most important message you want to get across? Don't be afraid to announce your job search right there. Some examples: Financial consultant specializing in travel price modeling; advertising executive looking to leverage event planning and social media skills; former lawyer looking to help environmentally focused nonprofits.

Draft an engaging, keyword-rich summary. You have fifty to one hundred words to make your pitch. Here you can briefly tell your professional story in a first-person, conversational voice. This is your opportunity to inject personality into the platform. Don't overly stress about this. Basic is better than nothing, and watch out for being overly sarcastic (mentioning you want to pivot from CEO of the household to CEO of someone else's household might garner you a few chuckles but you also risk alienating the more straitlaced recruiters).

Keep your job history short and sweet. You don't want to just cut and paste your resume into your LinkedIn profile—it should be a more concise version of your professional history. The best formats are a short summary statement with a few key highlights. And yes, include the dates of your prior jobs.

Highlight your extras. The beauty of LinkedIn is that you have the freedom to showcase what you think is most important about you. You aren't stuck with the conventional resume template. Look at options for adding sections like certifications, awards, languages. Share your own areas of expertise.

Get positive recommendations. If you don't already, aim to secure at least one recommendation for every job you've had. LinkedIn is all about social proof, and when recruiters or other contacts see that Joe loved working with you, it can reassure them that you're worth talking to. Recommendations tend to be a quid pro quo arrangement, so ask people who 1) will remember you and your work and 2) you would feel comfortable recommending as well. Get creative, too: your kid's school principal is a smart ask if you have worked closely with her. This is also a good opportunity to think about who should be on your reference hit list.

Turn on the "I'm seeking" functionality. If you want recruiters to be able to find you more easily, head to the "settings and privacy" section under your profile. Click on privacy, then scroll down to the "job seeking" category; toggle the "let recruiters know you're open to opportunities" feature to *yes*. This simple exercise will not only help you get in front of recruiters; it will also help put you in the mind-set to get ready to get down to business.

Once you feel good about your profile, start making connections. Consider uploading your contacts as a way to connect with people you know personally. You don't want to badger people or send connection requests to people you don't know without a personal note. Search for old colleagues or alumni. Explain why you're reaching out, how you're connected to the person, and your specific ask. Collecting connections for the sake of having connections will get you nowhere. Your profile also displays groups you're a part of, too, so it's a good idea to join relevant ones. Use the search bar at the top of LinkedIn to search for groups in your local area, as well as in your niche industry.

The amazing thing about LinkedIn is that your engagement on the site will have a direct translation to recruiters' perceptions of your intent. To reestablish your expertise, capitalize on the social platform to reengage with industry conversations. Share articles that are relevant and interesting, post your own content, like other people's updates—all these activities will appear on your profile. This can show that you're up on trends and paying attention to what's happening. It's easier than you think. Jen was standing in line at Starbucks when she read that Mary Tyler Moore died. The next thing she saw on Twitter, before she even ordered her latte, was a major university research study establishing that women in their twenties underplay their professional success to men because those men will be too intimidated to marry them. She was like, What?? The irony was palpable. So she quickly wrote an article to young women about why downplaying their successes was a huge mistake. She posted the article on Facebook, Twitter, and LinkedIn. The article got no traction on Facebook and Twitter but it got a lot of attention on LinkedIn. To date, the post has more than 100 comments, more than 1,000 likes, and more than 15,000 views. And that was all because Jen checked her Twitter feed while in line for coffee.

Now, to be fair, sometimes your post vanishes in a black hole. But sometimes what you're saying really resonates with people. For women who have taken a career break, LinkedIn can be your voice, your platform, and your chance to show the world that you're here, you're ready, you're skilled, and you're connected.

Demonstrate digital savvy beyond LinkedIn, too. It's no secret that all hiring managers google for background on potential candidates. Search yourself and see what comes up on page one. It's most likely your social profiles, so you will want to spend time updating your social media accounts to make sure they're most reflective of who you are right now. You don't need to make your Instagram public, especially if that's where you mainly share family photos, but you just want to be proactive about eliminating any red flags. Another smart tactic: buy your own name as a URL and set up a website or blog. It's so easy today using Squarespace or Wix. Keep it simple if you must, even with a big "Exciting things to come!" banner.

Step 4: Work your network.

This is a big one. We talk about networking a lot in this book for an obvious reason: these are the people who know you, can vouch for you, who want to see the best for you. People usually get jobs from people they know. A LinkedIn/Adler Group study found that 85 percent of jobs are filled through networking! It's the personal reference—the commonality that creates an instant connection and can move you one step closer to getting a job. The word *networking* in itself has such a negative connotation—instead think of networking as expanding your career circle.

Luck is what happens when preparation meets opportunity, a Roman philosopher said. The same can be said for successful networking. You're going to throw a hundred darts at the wall and maybe two will stick. But you only need one to stick to get a job. When we were starting our companies, collectively we probably reached out to 300 people, had 100+ coffee dates, which led to 50 more coffee dates, which led to a few key meetings with investors and clients. It's a ton of work, but you will learn from each of those experiences, whether it goes well or not. You also need to be ready to lead the conversation. You can't have the mind-set that you're going to meet someone and they're going to pave the way for you and hand you a job. Be prepared, be positive, be pleasant, be professional (dress the part), and don't be a pest (that last one really comes down to common sense). Always thank everyone who has helped you, no matter how big or small. Thank-yous go a long way and give you a favorable impression. Here's what else you need to do:

Take advantage of every moment and be present in that moment. Don't hide behind your laptop. Go to social gatherings with friends, professional events you find interesting, alumni events. Talk with others with interest about things that are interesting to you. Don't make every interaction a sale of what you want to do. Enjoy the opportunity to get together with others! Be curious and be interested in what people are saying. When she was in her twenties, Stacey went to dinner with her sister's best friend's parents. The woman's father ran a large fixed-income firm, so out of genuine curiosity and her training as a journalist, she just kept asking him a ton of questions. I'm not even sure I knew what fixed-income investment management really was at the time, but my genuine interest in what others do, how they got there, and what makes good businesses came through, Stacey says. He called about a week later and asked if I wanted to come work for them in a communications capacity. I did and he doubled my salary.

Have your pitch down. Are you prepared to talk about yourself as the rock star that you are? When they ask what's going on, recount your elevator pitch (in a casual way). You can even get feedback on it! Tell them you're starting the process of looking for a job and what you're interested in. If you still feel awkward or unsure about your goals, ask questions that'll keep them talking. Harvard Business School professors Alison Wood Brooks and Leslie K. John found that asking the right follow-up questions can achieve two major goals: information exchange (learning) and impression management (liking). "For job candidates, asking questions such as 'What am I not asking you that I should?' can signal competence, build rapport, and unlock key pieces of information about the position," they wrote in the *Harvard Business Review*. Asking good follow-up questions—ones that are casual in tone and open-ended—are powerful. "They signal to your conversation partner that you are listening, care, and want to know more," Brooks and John write. Stacey is proof of that; asking smart questions is how she got an unexpected job offer.

Networking is not just a chance for you to tell your story. It's a chance to learn more about other people and their career paths—the decisions they make, the passions they have. More talk leads to more action. Taking the time to meet with people will also help you figure out what you need to work on if you have been out for some time. Maybe someone will suggest a class for you to take? Or a conference to attend? Or another person in another industry for you to meet? They also might have good suggestions for ways you can make yourself more hireable.

Tell anyone who will listen that you are ready to head back. You never know who can help. Stacey's mom's career was relaunched when someone at a social gathering heard her talking about the stock market. Realize that the playground is the new old boys' club, with lots of networking opportunities—you can extend that concept to the soccer or basketball (name your kid's sport) sidelines. Think of every place you go as an opportunity to learn from someone you meet—and we don't mean in an overly aggressive way. When you're authentically connecting with other parents, learn more about their interests and work passions. You may be able to help one another down the road. You could tap your friend who was a creative director to help you create a website, or get freelance work from someone who just learned you are a proofreader on the side. Or you might wind up chatting with someone who is attending a cool seminar that sounds interesting to you. It's a long game.

Talk to the babysitter. Or anyone who is in a different circle or different generation than you, says Lindsey Pollak, author of *The Remix: How to Lead and Succeed in the Multigenerational Workplace*. She says that most people are unlikely to have a friend who is ten years older or younger than them, and at networking events (or any gathering really), our natural tendency is to talk to those who look similar to us. But by limiting your circle, you're limiting your opportunities. Pollak says she likes to ask her daughter's babysitters about what books they're reading or sites they love. It gets you in the habit of talking to different people from different backgrounds and learning more about what interests them.

Have a cheat sheet of icebreakers. Tiffany Dufu, author of *Drop the Ball*, and a self-described introvert, says, "I find the format of many events unconducive to genuinely getting to know people. Early in my career I discovered that if I imagined myself as a journalist in the middle of an interview, cocktail conversations became a lot less anxiety-provoking." Tiffany developed a set of questions to get people talking: What's your story (to warm them up)? What keeps you up at night? What are you most hopeful about these days? Or, If you could go back in time and give yourself advice, what period in your life would you go back to and what would you tell yourself? The key is to just keep them talking. "The best result of this approach is that 1) the person will like you and trust you more after they've just opened up to you and 2) you'll learn everything you'll need to know about how you might want to engage them in the future, either for business or as a friend," says Dufu.

Have an agenda or specific goal for your conversation. When you set up coffee dates or calls with old colleagues or friends who have made the transition back to work, remember time is a valuable priority and you don't want to waste the opportunity to gain insight or a reference. What are you most hoping to gain from this particular person? Advice on companies to look into? People they might know who are hiring? General advice on your industry? Let them know what you're looking for. Say, "Can I buy you coffee? I'd love to hear your opinion on X." That's Jen's go-to line. Don't say, "Can I pick your brain?" Or, "I'm at a loss. Can I talk to you?" Yes, people like to help—they like to hear that you need help. But they also don't want you to waste their time, so you want to be as detailed as possible when you ask something of them.

Set goals and parameters for yourself. Maybe you will connect with two people, one company, and attend one event every week. Find the events that naturally work with your lifestyle. Don't assume you can't network because you can't make it out at night. Drink and dinner dates are hard for many women whose partners have an extreme travel schedule or who simply don't want to miss bedtime. Instead, create a schedule that works for you—plan breakfast meetings and coffee dates, and pepper in an evening event when you can. Look for companies hosting recruiting events during the day.

Other great places to expand your network: Connect with alumni from your college or graduate school. You can find those groups on LinkedIn or Facebook, or even through the university itself. Twitter chats are also low-stakes opportunities to join a conversation. You can post something on your community Facebook mom groups, too. Today there are many powerful women's groups on Facebook that allow you to post that you're looking for a job: Moms in Tech, Women in Product (WIP), or the PR, Marketing, and Media Czars. Or just post a note to your own Facebook profile and let the friend hive respond. Just ask Jacinta Chadwick, who cast a wide net when looking to return to work but found "it was an uphill battle convincing recruiters and companies to see past my six-year career pause." She posted her interest in returning to work on Facebook, and landed a job . . . at Facebook! After six months she transitioned from contractor to full-time employee.

Informational interviews are another good tactic to get your foot in the door. Do your research, find out who you want to speak to within the company, contact that person, and ask for time to meet. You might be surprised how often people are willing to say yes. Networking can be incredibly time consuming—you might find yourself wishing people would actually say no!

Lastly, keep the connections going by finding opportunities to reciprocate. It often feels like you're asking for favors, but if you can think about how you can help someone out, that is, send an article of interest to them, introduce them to someone that might help them, or send them a congratulatory letter when they have professional success, you will likely build an enduring relationship. This process is about reinvigorating your old network, tapping into the relationships you've made while on your break, and fueling new connections to take you to the nitty-gritty of getting the job.

Employers want good, solid, energetic people. Friends want to recommend people who are going to reflect favorably on themselves. Beyond your skills and resume points, the most important thing is to establish that you're enthusiastic, human, and someone who would be great to work with. At the end of the day, the gap will fade away.

HOW COMPANIES CAN SHINE:
Recognize unconscious bias.

Motherhood discrimination and bias exists, beginning with hiring through employment and long before people became part of the work world. Examining your practices and how to change them is critical to decreasing this bias. Research shows that resumes of nonmothers receive 2.1 times the callbacks of mothers, and that job queries from women and people of color are far more likely to be ignored and requests for meetings denied.

"Humans rely on something called heuristics to assist in quick decision making, which is just a technical term for unconscious," says Daisy Auger-Dominguez, a diversity and inclusion leadership expert. "Decades of research by social scientists make it clear that our brains take these shortcuts to conclusions without telling us. Despite clarity on the business case, our good intentions and our desire to be fair and merit-based in our assessments of others, our unconscious biases create blind spots." Companies need to start interviewing all candidates without bias. Here's how:

1. **Conduct unconscious bias training for hiring managers.** The fact is, we all have unconscious bias and proper training helps us recognize the bias and ensure we don't make decisions based on often incorrect reasoning. Companies should regularly provide effective unconscious bias training, especially for hiring managers. Educate this group on the benefits of people who have taken career breaks. Take a hard, realistic look around your leadership—are there women? Are there mothers? Train leadership on why gender diversity is so important and why hiring people of different backgrounds and experiences is critical to the company's success. Teach them to value caregiving years, not dismiss them.

2. **Hire a diversity and inclusion lead or create an internal task force.** We know that while companies are putting an emphasis on workplace culture, pay equity, and diversity and inclusion, very little is changing. For example, in 2014, Silicon Valley began publishing diversity reports to provide more transparency into its workforce and pledged to do better. Five

years on, the numbers are still largely the same. Companies must create ownership of D & I goals across the company and focus on efforts to commit to develop and promote more women to senior levels.

3. **Review your job descriptions, plus your hiring and interview policies.** Consider applicant sources and be wary of just relying on referrals only to find good talent, which inevitably promotes homogeneity. Implement the Rooney Rule to source diverse candidates. Invest in software that will anonymize resumes and remove masculine words from your job listing and include information about culture. Interview questions should be limited to the person's ability to perform the job that is available, and the same general set of questions should be used for *every* applicant.

CHAPTER 9

GET IN THE JOB SEARCH GAME

You are ready for this! You've spent time and energy perfecting your resume and your elevator pitch. You even have a five-star LinkedIn profile. All of this preparation has had a larger impact on you than you might realize. You're a bit more at ease talking about your goals of returning to work. You hopefully have more clarity on what you want to do. You are now ready to sell yourself to a potential new employer. Now you need to get to the brass tacks of looking for the right job and prepping for the interview.

You may be a little nervous about this next step, which is absolutely exactly how you should be feeling. But remember this—a potential employer is looking for one thing: a reliable, good, loyal employee. Also, keep in mind that hiring managers have a really difficult job—they are real people who are trying to suss out who is the right fit for the job. They're not there to probe into your life and career decisions or judge you for them. If you get grilled it's only to assess how well you react to a pressure-filled situation, and trust us, you're prepared for those.

This is also your decision as much as it is theirs. Go into

the process knowing that you're vetting potential employers, too. Just like in dating, it needs to be a good match. You don't want someone who doesn't value you and your experience. If you feel like you're apologizing for your choices, the company won't be a good fit for you as much as you won't be a good fit for it.

A key tactic: get organized. Looking for a job can be a full-time job. While you're networking, sending resumes, and going on interviews, it is important to be methodical about keeping track of your activity so you can follow up and stay connected with your contacts. Stephanie Won said, "I tracked my job search like a marketing campaign in a spreadsheet that I updated religiously every Sunday night, constantly measuring and evaluating my return on investment of time in all the activities." Be realistic: you want to devote as much time as possible to your job search, but while you're in this transition phase, without the backup care that most working parents rely on, you need to be strategic with your time.

Each day, build out a task list and timeline. Perhaps you have four hours of alone time each day. Divide that between job search tasks and "me time," allowing the remaining hours to be for the kids or family activities. Each day, ask yourself, "What is most important to complete today for the job search, for the family, for me time?" Give yourself a goal to hit every day to keep you on track, whether it's reaching out to one new person or applying to a job, and try to appreciate this transition time. Having a support system is undeniably a smart strategy. Your return-to-work squad will help keep you on track—with them you can share war stories and remind each other to laugh.

While the emotions can feel overwhelming, once you do get the offer (and you will!) this period will be long forgotten. It's like childbirth. No one remembers that, right?

Apply Yourself

To streamline your search, first think about your own requirements. Is it location? Type of role? Type of company? Number of hours/work arrangement? Salary? Write them all down in priority order; this will dictate the key words you will use to search for jobs. Read job descriptions carefully, but don't get bogged down by qualifications or requirements. Someone had the task of writing a job description, but that is often merely a starting point. Most good companies are intent on hiring the best person, even if she has ten years more experience than what is listed. Remember, don't fall into that statistic that women think they need to meet 100 percent of the requirements to apply for a job.

Tailor your resume for each type of role you're applying to. You don't need to have one hundred different versions of your resume, but look at the job descriptions and lists of responsibilities of the jobs you are considering. In your prior experience, customize your accomplishments to hit these points. Even if it's not a one-for-one match (for example, success with marketing campaigns) don't let that dissuade you from applying for the job. Skills can be transferable and you most likely have talents that align with what the hiring manager is looking for. For example, if you're interested in a marketing role, what experience do you have, either past or during your gap, where you used your communication and social media skills to get the job done? Maybe for a fund-raiser you created a Facebook page to market the event to a larger community. Include that as an impact-oriented bullet point (for example, grew the school's Facebook page by X percent).

Depending on what industry you are applying to, listing recent continuing education and certifications and your software literacy (for example, proficient in Excel, Slack, etc.) can show your job readiness and ease hiring managers' concerns.

Also, don't let the technical jargon scare you away. Job descriptions may ask if you have experience with CRM platforms (that's email/newsletters), Trello (project management software), or SCRUM (agile product development). Google the terms you don't know. If there seems to be a common software requirement that you're not familiar with, look for classes or online tutorials that teach these skills. If you're not up for a class, or require just a few hours of brushing up, use your network to locate a connection that is willing to spend an afternoon walking you through the software you need to know. Ask your industry friends what they're using and take the time to learn about them. Many companies, especially start-ups, rely on Google Docs. Familiarize yourself with them all so you know what you're talking about in interviews.

In reading descriptions, ask yourself, would you feel inspired and engaged in this role? How would it challenge you? It's natural to just want to get a job and not worry too much about it being the perfect role. Often, you may not have a choice, either. But if you can check off some of your priority boxes, you are more likely to reenter happier and more motivated. If you're interested, feel that you could do the job, and it meets your lifestyle needs, go for it.

Sometimes you need an extra push to apply. We know this intimately thanks to handling customer service for Après as a way to stay in touch with users. Women reach out regularly with questions about whether to apply even though they may not meet all the requirements. The problem with not applying is that no one will ever see your resume if you don't. So we answer questions and encourage—we're the cheerleaders behind the scenes.

To better your odds, if there's a job open at a company you're interested in, search to see if anyone in that company has a connection to you. For example, is there a fellow school alum at the company? Is there someone who shares the same interests as you? Try to find any common connections and then use that connection by sending that person your resume. You want some way to get your resume on the top of the pile. As we said earlier, keep an organized spreadsheet of what you've applied to and the status—especially if it's through a human connection. You want to follow up in an appropriate manner. There's a fine line between showing interest and being annoying—the best guideline is to touch base seven days after you apply.

A note about cover letters: they seem antiquated but many companies still ask for them. You'll want to mention 1) how you learned of the job, whether you saw a posting or through a specific person; 2) what excites you about the job; and 3) what you bring to the table for this job specifically. No one reads long emails. Keep this short and sweet and get ready for the interview requests to come pouring in!

A common complaint we hear is when an applicant does not receive any response from a company after submitting a resume. Do not take this silence to heart. Again, hiring managers are usually hiring for multiple positions and vetting hundreds of resumes. We always recommend waiting at least one week before sending a short email to check in. If possible, send along an article or something of interest in this email as an excuse to check in. Do not appear irritated or insulted by the lack of the company's response. Just keep moving forward.

Prepare for Interviews

Interviews are always nerve-racking. In fact, 92 percent of Americans admit to being extremely anxious about job interviews, according to a Harris Interactive and Everest College poll. That same study found that not knowing the answer to an interviewer's question and being overqualified were respondents' two largest interview fears. There's nothing you can do about feeling overqualified—that's just a reality you may have to face from time to time (see our sidebar of Tricky Interview Questions on page 208 for how to answer that one). But being extra prepared can eliminate the stumped factor.

Define your intentions. Why do you want this position? What attracted you to it? Be very honest with yourself. Is it the flexibility? Title? Company? Maybe it just sounded cool? You will be asked what interested you about this job and you want to have a clear sense of what it is about the job that you are most excited about. Frame it positively and in corporate speak. Don't say because it's part-time and I have to be home by 3 p.m. Instead say that your research on the company has led you to believe the company has worked hard to create a great culture, and working for a company that cares about its culture and its employees is important to you.

Be ready with your strengths and weaknesses. As you prepare for an interview, read the job posting carefully to determine what skills or strengths are most valued. If it's a project manager role, stating your organizational skills and ability to collaborate with multiple stakeholders is a good start. You will most likely be asked about weaknesses, too. Answers like "I'm a perfectionist" or "I have a hard time saying no" are ubiquitous. Instead, really think of a weakness that's fixable with a corresponding story you can tell. The example career coach Carroll Welch gives: "I tend to be overly critical of myself. In my last role at a nonprofit, my boss, who was also my mentor, saw this trait as an impediment to my supervising younger colleagues and pointed it out. I worked on some strategies to address this and subsequently was asked to run the training program for new hires."

Never make fun of yourself, your age, or your experience. This is the most important rule, especially if you're interviewing with someone younger than you. Lindsey Pollak, author of *The Remix: How to Lead and Succeed in the Multigenerational Workplace,* advises applicants to never say:

- "I'm such a Luddite."
- "You could be my daughter."
- "Back in my day . . ."
- "We used to call it . . ."
- "I don't know because I was a manager when you were in diapers!"

These are obvious, we hope, but the main takeaway is to not call out an age difference ever in an interview. Don't dwell or criticize yourself. Instead say, yes, I took X years off to raise my kids and now I'm back. You can bond with people age eighteen or eighty if you share the same passion or have something professional in common.

Research the company. What is the culture like? What do they believe in? Does the CEO/founder speak publicly about any issues? Do you know who your boss would be? To answer these, you can research on the Web, look at sites like Glassdoor, or look on LinkedIn for anyone you know who works or has worked there. "The importance of prep work and doing your homework for interviews or networking is undeniable," says Pollak. If you're applying for a job at Rent the Runway, have you downloaded the app? Do you use the service? "I don't care if you've been out of the workforce for ten years. If you're a genuine fan of a company's work, if you speak someone else's language, that's sometimes all the bond and connection you need," she says. Know what's important to the people you are interviewing with—read their Twitter feed. What drives them? Doing the prep work will prove you're genuinely interested in and knowledgeable about the work.

Build your signature story. Once you understand more about the job and the company, craft the story in your head of how you match to them. Be ready to answer the questions: How will you add value to the company? Why is the culture a good fit for your values? Once you have these talking points, you will be able to authentically explain why this role is important to you and how your skills, interests, and talents are well aligned. Fran Hauser, author of *The Myth of the Nice Girl*, recommends having your top three talking points at the ready and being able to weave them into the conversation no matter what has been asked. It can be about your talents, about why you want this job, or the added value you'll provide to the company if you are hired.

Listen to the interviewer's questions. You may be thinking this is obvious, but we hear this complaint from hiring managers all the time. You may be so anxious to get out your story that you ignore what the interviewer is asking! Don't make this mistake. The ability to listen is an important trait for any good employee. Establish this in your interview.

Get ready for standard questions. "Tell me about yourself" or "Why are you interested in this job?" will most likely be the icebreaker. Do not recite your resume or job history. Tell a story that fills in the blanks and explains the why behind all the bullet points. What motivates you, what are you passionate about? Set yourself apart with these answers. We always suggest practicing your first few sentences verbatim—over and over and over again. The first few minutes of an interview are the toughest and if you feel really prepared for your opening, the rest of the interview will fall into place.

There will be other signature questions (Why you? What is something you're proud of? What is a challenge you had and how did you solve it? What is something you bring to the table that no other applicant does?) There will be tricky questions (What have you been doing?). There might even be puzzles, a practice common at big tech companies. Practice with your partner or friends. This is the best way to get comfortable with your answers. If you put a college award for a paper you wrote on your resume, you'd better be prepared to discuss it in detail. That's what happened to one woman who was totally taken by surprise when asked about her college thesis. But it was right there at the end of her resume!

Be mindful of your body language. If you've heard that 93 percent of communication is nonverbal, this is why: In 1967, researcher and current professor emeritus of psychology at the University of California, Los Angeles, Albert Mehrabian and a group of colleagues that studied body language introduced the 7%–38%–55% Rule. It stands for the impact of words, tone of voice, and body language when speaking. Basically, what you say is only a small part of what you're being judged on. You want to make sure you sit up straight, make eye contact, and don't fidget. Exuding confidence is your best asset to getting a job.

Prepare your own questions. Employers expect you to ask your own questions—this gives them insight into what matters most to you. And remember, you *want* this opportunity to find out if it is a good place for you, too. You most likely left your job all those years ago because it wasn't. If this is your first interview, don't interrogate the person about the ins and outs of their family policies. Raising the topic of flexibility too early in the process may look like you're more concerned about what's right for you, rather than showing what value you bring to the company. Instead, ask general questions like "Can you tell me about the culture here? What do you like about working here?" That may answer your questions without directly stating them. It can be tricky to figure out at what point should you ask specifically about flexibility, especially if this is a nonnegotiable for you. Our advice: wait until you have an offer in hand.

Practice, practice, practice. Ask a friend to conduct a mock interview with you and even consider video-recording it—observe how you behave, what you say, and try to improve upon any quirks you might have. Also, a hiring manager might ask to have a video call instead. Test out the software ahead of time to work out the technical kinks to make sure your volume sounds good, your picture is clear, and your background image is appropriate (don't do it from the couch in a messy living room).

Dress to impress. Wardrobe anxiety is one of the most common fears we hear about. Every industry has its own secret dress code, so your best bet is to talk to friends who work in similar roles and ask them what the vibe is like in their office. For instance, you should wear a suit to an interview at a traditional financial institution, but that might come across as out-of-touch at a tech start-up. When in doubt: a nice pair of pants, heels, and a fun blouse and maybe a blazer does the trick. Or a simple sheath dress. You never want to come across as too casual—you want to feel like you, but the polished, I'm ready for work, version.

In the end, always follow up with a thank-you note. Send an email within hours of an interview. A handwritten note is not essential, unless someone really went above and beyond for you. You want to leave the door open and a positive impression even if you don't receive an offer.

ANSWERS TO TRICKY INTERVIEW QUESTIONS

How will you balance work and family obligations?

"My whole family is supportive of my decision to get back to my career and everyone is prepared to do what is necessary to make it work."

OR

"I took time off to care for a relative who is now in an assisted living facility and well cared for."

Do you feel that your professional skills are up-to-date?

"Over the past couple of years I've done freelance work, taken online courses, and attended workshops. I've maintained my skills and expertise by reading, attending industry events, and donating time to charitable organizations that needed volunteers with my qualifications."

Why did you leave your last job?

"I resigned from my last job to be my children's primary caregiver. I'm now ready to reenter the workforce and contribute to your company in the following ways."

You seem overqualified for the job. Why should we hire you?

"This is the level and position that I want and specifically sought out your company. I am confident that I can succeed in the role and become more valuable to you sooner."

How do you feel reporting to someone with less experience?

"A good manager has the knowledge and ability to bring out the best in their people, regardless of age or years of experience."

Why are you changing careers?

> *"While I have been home, I have been active in the PTA over the past five years. Over the last two years I took on the officer role of treasurer, managing a twenty-thousand-dollar budget and collaborating with school leaders and parents. I've learned a lot working in education and am excited to transition to an accounting role in an academic institution."*

OR

> *"I've been involved with XYZ charitable organization for four years and successfully led their big fund-raiser the past two years. I am looking to apply my project management and people management skills as an event manager working for an organization that is committed to helping people in the community."*

Sussing Out Good Boss Potential

There's a common career adage that you should pick your boss, not your job. Here's why it's true: company policies—and their bent toward being more or less flexible—will vary, but if you develop a good relationship with your manager (and you're good at your job), you will be in a much stronger place to cultivate the work environment you desire. If you have a boss like Stacey's at the *Wall Street Journal*, who knew what it was like to balance kids and the need to work a less traditional schedule, it will eliminate that feeling of guilt and sneaking around for a doctor's appointment. But, let's be honest, there are definitely people who don't quite get the fact that you have another full-time unpaid job outside the workplace.

It's hard to know for certain until you actually work together, but during your interview attempt to get a glimpse into the type of boss you may have on your hands. Ask questions to better understand his or her management style, read between the lines, and study the emotional cues. Is she talking about herself a lot instead of the team? Is he letting you complete your answers or is he constantly interrupting? Is she grilling you, or is she more welcoming and open to introducing you to other people on the team? In her *Harvard Business Review* article, Priscilla Claman, president of Career Strategies Inc., recommends asking these questions:

- Is there someone working for you that you consider a real star that I could learn from? The goal here is to really understand what he or she values in an employee.
- Can you tell me about a recent project the team completed and how it went? Ask for specifics to glean how involved the manager was in the process.
- What are the typical customers like or what is the team like? This will give you a sense of the manager's feelings toward others and how he or she treats them.
- How would you describe the culture here? See if the responses are similar to "family friendly," "welcoming," "collaborative," or, alternatively, "competitive," "results driven," "intense."

This is a really high proverbial tightrope to walk. As someone returning to the workforce, you must project a strong commitment to returning to work and not appear to be asking for special treatment in an interview.

What has your interaction been like after the interview? Trust your gut. Look, we have all had bad bosses. While you can't be overly picky, you also want to be certain you're making a smart decision as you go into the negotiation process.

How to Find a Good Company

"What kind of company will even hire me?"

This is the other question that fills our in-boxes. First, remember, there are tons of companies always looking for help, like in retail and tech. According to Tina Lee, founder of MotherCoders, there is a real dearth of women holding technical roles across all industries. Her nonprofit is changing this through an innovative tech training model specifically designed for moms. Over nine weeks, moms learn coding skills in front-end Web development, gain industry knowledge, and develop a support network to help them jump-start new careers in tech. Big companies and forward-thinking cities are taking note—Google recently sponsored a MotherCoders boot camp in New York with support from women.nyc. Get this—all MC boot camps include on-site child care.

The good news is that there are companies out there specifically looking for people who have taken career breaks. It is far from perfect, but more and more companies are wising up to the need to be more open-minded toward employment gaps. There are ways to identify companies that are favorable toward working parents and just a darn good place to work.

Go online and look at the website of a company that you're dying to work at. Look for returnships or training opportunities, benefits and leave policies, as well as some lesser-known programs that can give you a clue as to what the company values and what the culture is like, which together will help you figure out what matters most to you in a job. Here are some areas to research:

Paid leave: Does the company offer paid leave? Stacey was talking to a group of women looking to get back into the workforce, and the topic turned to paid leave at companies—if they offer it or not, and how much. She noticed it was falling largely on deaf ears. We get it. These women have had their kids and raised them for many years—in some cases into middle school and high school. Their worries are in a different direction as they try to return to work. They need creative ways to refresh their resumes or for a hiring manager to overlook a gap on the resume. They may need new skills or someone to take a chance on them.

That said, we should all care if a company offers paid leave—whether you're about to graduate from college or from that MBA program and not quite ready for children, or if your children are grown. A company that offers employees paid leave is a company you want to work for because they've put time, thought, and money into a policy that wants to attract and retain female talent. It's an even better signal if the company is offering paid leave for men or has moved to an overall "paid leave" approach for all new parents, including those who adopt. Those companies are also contributing to breaking down gender-specific roles, and their paid leave policy could be an indicator that they're progressive in other ways, too, when it comes to creating a corporate infrastructure that's designed to support its employees. In fact, 34 percent of companies that offer paid leave *also offer* some form of flexible work and child-care options.

Backup child-care offerings: Every kid gets sick a few times a year. In order to keep the world spinning, you need to have a backup plan. Many employers offer backup child-care programs where employees could tap into either on-site child care or a vetted network of independent care professionals.

Corporate social responsibility programs: How does the business's practices benefit society? This can mean everything from donating a portion of annual profits to charity to adopting eco-friendly initiatives. This gives you a glimpse into the values and purpose of the company itself.

Bereavement time: At MassMutual, employees are granted fourteen days of paid leave to grieve a loved one. This shows that the company values their employees' well-being—and recognizes that sometimes life (or death) happens.

Global offices: Where are the majority of the employees located? Are they bicoastal? Bicontinental? Collaboration technology has allowed for a geographically diverse workforce (and the easing of a strict nine-to-five workday), but if the majority of the team is in California it might require a ton of travel or a shift in "regular" hours. What time zone is the executive team located in? Little things like this can tell you a lot about when you might need to be available for calls. Remember, too much travel is what nearly broke Jen the first time around.

Work policies and cultural cues can either catapult your career with kids or stop you in your tracks. No matter what life stage you're in, look closely at the company where you're working or thinking of accepting an offer from. Don't go into something blind; look around, look at who's making up the company; ask to talk to women who work there. Does it represent a place that makes sense for you to work? Do your research: Companies have a lot of great policies, but are people taking advantage of them? Do they get penalized for taking them?

So, how can you really tell what it's like to work at a company? Watch for these signs in informational meetings or interviews:

1. Is the company proud of its culture? Do they work hard to ensure their employees are happy and their needs are met? Are they talking about it in the interview?

2. How do they talk about the business? Are people trying to "kill it" or "crush it"? Or do they say that winning and outdoing each other doesn't matter?

3. How they talk about life outside work: Are employees valued for volunteer work or if they serve on boards?

4. Do you see any company swag lying around? Do they seem appropriate for men *and* women: not just logo-laden flasks, leather jackets, and XXL T-shirts given out at golf courses. Are there actually female-cut T-shirts and non-sports-focused company events?

5. How do they speak about the other women in the office in leadership roles (if there are any!)?

6. Has the company been in the news for good or for bad about diversity and inclusion policies and practices in general, that is, #MeToo, paid leave, discrimination? Google the company to see if it or any of its executives have been in the press. While it can be difficult to really know if a company has an inherently negative or bro culture, in the era of #MeToo, thankfully, voices are coming forward to shed light on horrific practices and harassing behavior.

Be Honest with Yourself

You need to think about what you can offer. In order to be successful at your job, you need to be honest about what kind of job commitment you can handle. Can you work a full-time schedule? What about commuting? Do you really need to stay local? If the company says, "There may be some travel," can you do it? While job parameters do change and there is always room for negotiation, be reasonable. If your needs are completely opposite of what's being offered, it's not going to be the right role for you.

Here's the good news. Many workplaces are more flexible than in the past, and there is a steady rise in the number of people who work at home, about 8 million, according to the U.S. Census. In part, we have the younger generation to thank for this. Research from Werk shows that millennials are taking on caretaker roles and spending an average of twenty-one hours a week assisting a parent, grandparent, or sibling. This is driving the need for flexibility to the top of job-hunt requirements. It's also an olive branch to shared space workers who don't operate as efficiently with distraction at a level nine. Managers get it: neighbors are just an arm's length away, and there's little space for storing your commuting shoes—or organizing your thoughts.

"There is such a need for flexibility for people at all stages of their careers, entry to exec level," says Sara Sutton, founder of FlexJobs. "It's not just a warm-and-fuzzy policy—people need work flexibility at some point in their career, whether to take care of a loved one who is ill, or yourself, or to temper a long, stressful commute. It's the way of the future—the demand for flexibility will only rise." Her site lists the best industries for working on your own terms:

- Sales
- Computer and IT
- Medical and Health
- Customer Service
- Education and Training
- Account/Project Management
- Administrative

- Accounting and Finance
- Marketing
- HR and Recruiting

Technology, and its ability to allow professionals to work remotely, is why most of these categories top the list. It's also the nature of the roles. Sales, for instance, is a very autonomous role where you are responsible for making the deals how you best see fit. Others, like project management or even in the health care and education field, rely on project-based workers, fill-ins, and substitutes to get the job done. They know that your work output is the most important priority—not necessarily where or how much you do it. Trust is implicit. Trust is everything.

One senior manager told us, "My first employer did everything right—I had a ton of trust and flexibility, amazingly equipped mothers' room (couch! sink! microwave! fridge! even a board with pics of our babies and dish soap and brushes!). The employer I went to next, by contrast, did everything wrong. I had no time nor place to pump, even though the business provided lactation consulting. The stress was toxic and unbearable. The demands were unreasonable for most people, let alone a new mom."

Ask the right questions and you will get the answers. If that senior manager had talked to another new mom, she may have learned that the lactation consultant was just lip service. One of the reasons Jen took the job at Epstein was that during the interview process they were very receptive to her inquiries about gender diversity and culture. But it can be tricky to ask the questions in a way that doesn't make anyone defensive or penalize you for inquiring about it. It's all in how you phrase it. Instead of: Do you have family-friendly policies? Ask, How are you supportive of employees? If you're nervous to ask to meet with senior female leaders, say this: "For me, at the very top of my list is a great culture and I want to be around people I like working with and who like working at the company. Would it be possible for me to speak to other people at the company, maybe some women?"

If they are weird about it, there's your answer. If they're happy to, there is your answer.

Is it a male-dominated culture? Remember, double standards do exist. When a man walks through an airport with three kids, most people will go out of their way to help "the poor soul." When a woman does the same, it's just any other day. You would think at work it would be the reverse—that a woman, who makes it to a client meeting after packing lunches, dropping the kids off at school, and fielding calls from the babysitter, would be applauded each and every day. And there are some companies that do. Finding an office with women and men who are committed to gender diversity and supporting the pipeline of more female talent is important.

The best test, we will say it again, is to just look around. What do you see? Do you see yourself there? What is the vibe you get in the office and from the people there? Trust your gut.

Here's another little secret: start-ups and small businesses are often more willing to take a risk on you. Start-ups need people to take a chance on them—often, people aren't willing to leave their more stable jobs for a vision. They are seeking the best talent, and often don't hold on to antiquated notions of hierarchy. They also need people to get things done—stat. That's why it's a great place for people who are looking to revive their careers. That's what happened to Susan Levitt. Susan, a former director in Citigroup's Capital Markets Division, took a six-year break from the corporate world. She became an active member of her kids' school board and was happy during this time. Then, before she knew it, her kids had grown up and "didn't seem to need me as much anymore," Susan says. She started looking around for jobs in the financial industry again, and she was surprised where she eventually found herself: at a start-up. That startup was Kroll Bond Rating Agency and the leap of faith paid off for everyone. "I had the right background and experience, so they took a gamble on me. I was hired as the tenth employee, hired to run business development, and now I still run business development for a team of a hundred-plus people."

You will find your club. Find a company that welcomes that club. It will help you survive the Messy Middle.

Quiz: Is Your Workplace Truly Family Friendly?

Do yourself a favor: look around ask about these policies before you really need them. And even if you don't need all of them—if you're beyond child-bearing years, knowing that a company offers a paid leave benefit will tell you so much about the company and its evolution to be a company that supports women and working families. Just 13 percent of the population has access to paid leave at all. The companies that are offering paid leave are much further ahead than others and are likely much further ahead in thinking about benefits to keep women talent from leaving.

So what benefits really matter? Here's a little scavenger hunt for you:

1. Find out the number of weeks of paid family leave—not the number of Ping-Pong tournaments (though those are fun, too).

2. Ask how many men have taken more than two weeks for paternity leave.

3. Count the number of women in leadership roles.

4. Count the number of women in leadership roles who have kids.

5. Count the number of women in leadership roles who have kids and whom you would consider role models.

6. Count the number of eye-rolls a woman gets for leaving work "early" to relieve the sitter.

7. Count the number of times a woman gets "manterrupted" in a meeting.

8. Count the number of work trips you have to take in a given month. Trust us, they get tougher and tougher.

9. Scan the company's marketing and PR language. Bonus points for commitments to professional development, equal pay, and gender diversity.

10. Explore whether the company supports a women's group or women's initiatives.

Negotiate for What You Want

You got a job offer! Now it's time to ask for a salary you feel good about. For someone who has endured months of coffee dates, unanswered emails, confusion, and rejection, your first inclination is probably to shout "Yes, yes, yes!" to the first job offer you receive. But take a moment to really think about the job and what they are proposing. Don't let the fact that you've been on the career sidelines trump your power to negotiate and your desire for a job you're excited about. It doesn't have to be *the* job, but it should be one that you could be happy about for at least six months.

The reality is women don't negotiate nearly as often as men. One study of MBA students who were applying for their first jobs after graduation found that only one-eighth of the women negotiated, while more than half of the men did. It's often due to a fear of social backlash: research has shown that male and female leaders "were less interested in working with women who attempted to negotiate a better salary." And for returners who are simply thankful that they have a job offer in hand, their predominant fear is that they will jeopardize the offer and come across as overly demanding.

We understand, bias is real. But you need to not let it affect your mind-set. It *is* possible to negotiate a salary commensurate with your skill set and experience and feel good about doing it. Don't assume that your salary will suffer compared to others in similar roles simply because you took a career break, but understand that your salary may be adjusted because there's an assumption that your on-ramp into the role may take longer than someone who hasn't taken a break. Our advice: be fair to yourself and be realistic. Remember, you were chosen for this job for a reason—a very good reason! So don't ever accept the first offer. Here's how to make your case.

Do your research. Take your career break out of the equation and just look for what the salary range is for the exact job you will be doing. Check PayScale and Glassdoor for competitive salary information. Talk to your network and ask their perspective on your value in the workplace. You might be getting paid less than you were making at your last job before you took a break, but don't let this get you down. Focus on a fair salary for the job you will be doing—and maybe add in a few extra dollars for your extra experience. The more data you have to support your ask, the more likely you will get to yes. You can say, I talked to people in the industry and learned that the salary range is closer to X. Would you consider increasing the offer to Y?

Practice what you're going to say. Have your talking points at the ready and think about someone else when you're talking. Research shows that women are more successful in negotiations when they're negotiating on behalf of someone else.

Consider other benefits instead of salary. What are the nonnegotiables for you?

After spending more than twenty years in human resources in corporate America, sandwiched by a brief stint as a consultant, Elizabeth Scott knows what she really wants out of her next job: the ability to work a full-time but flexible schedule. Scott, whose boys are seven and eight years old, set some personal boundaries for herself as she considers her next role: the ability to drive car pool one day a week, be home for dinner, be emotionally present. But when do you ask for flex time? We do not recommend requesting an accommodation during the interview, especially if you do not know the company policies. Julie Casson, global director of marketing at Inbenta, raised her desire to work from home on Fridays after several meetings when they started to discuss terms of an offer. "I was a bit nervous bringing it up as a bottom-line factor, but I am so glad that I spoke up about my needs. And I was rewarded by having it granted!" There is no perfect time, but during the negotiation process is the safest place to start.

Consider what will happen if you get a no. When do you feel good about walking away? It depends on how the process went. If it was a really negative experience, then this might not be the best company for you. And there is a sense of power (and a boost in confidence) if you pass on an offer that is simply not up to snuff. But if you like the company and think it would be a great fit, you may consider agreeing to a slightly lower salary or a nonflexible schedule, but ask if it's possible to revisit the issue in six months—after you've proven your merit as a new employee. Some companies, like Viacom, grant flexible schedules to employees who have been there for a certain amount of time. Or, if you didn't get the exact salary you wanted, ask for a performance-based bonus if you hit a certain agreed-upon milestone, such as growth in business revenue, fund-raising dollars, or money saved. Just because the negotiations are over, it doesn't mean you can't revisit your wants in a few months.

The other challenge you may face: your start date. Employers will want you ASAP. If you are home with your kids, you will need time to deal with plenty of logistics (hello, child care!) and mentally prepare yourself to be a working parent again. Without divulging specifics, don't be afraid to make your employer wait. Not an eternity, of course, but at least two to three weeks to begin to ease your family into the transition and to mentally prepare yourself to jump into the working world again.

HOW COMPANIES CAN SHINE:
Pay people equally.

Every year in April, on Equal Pay Day, we are reminded of the gender pay gap between women and men: right now, women earn $0.78 cents for every dollar a man makes, and mothers who work full-time, year-round make just $0.71 cents of what fathers working the same amount make. Single mothers working full-time and year-round fare the worst—earning $0.58 cents for every dollar that fathers earn working the same amount. Asian American working mothers earn slightly more than all working mothers ($0.74 cents per dollar) compared to white working mothers ($0.71), African American working mothers ($0.54), and Latina working mothers ($0.49). These sobering statistics barely budge from year to year, and it's frankly sad that we need a day to raise awareness about a topic that should be a nontopic—because women should be paid the same as men. Period. Companies can change this financial roadblock. Here's how:

1. **Promote pay transparency at your company.** Do women in the same role as men make the same salary at your company? In 2015, two women at Salesforce asked this question and proposed to CEO Marc Benioff that the company conduct an audit of employee salaries to find out. The subsequent equal pay initiative resulted in Salesforce spending $3 million to equalize pay for about 6 percent of 17,000 salaries across function, level, and location. Buffer, a social media company, publishes what everyone makes publicly as a way to stay on top of the pay gap.

2. **Support federal policies that work to bridge the pay gap.** The impact of the gap, and what is essentially lower wages, affects not just women, but also their families and the economy. For example, if the gap were closed, the National Partnership for Women & Families (NPWF) reports, a woman could afford 15 more months of child care, 78 more weeks of food for her family, and more. Educate yourself and your employees

about policy efforts that could fight bias and address fair pay, including family-friendly workplace standards, and the Paycheck Fairness Act.

3. **Offer women returning to work fair salaries.** Yes, they have taken a break. But don't penalize them in a paycheck. Offer a fair salary for the role being offered and not a penny less.

CHAPTER 10

HOW TO OWN YOUR ROLE AS A WORKING PARENT (AGAIN)

Welcome back! It wasn't easy and it wasn't always fun, but you did it—you landed that job. You will be excited, nervous, proud, and scared all at the same time. But most important, you will feel alive and energized by the challenges ahead. One of those is preparing your home team for your new role.

Going back to work is a big change for you and likely a very big one for your family. The simple fact is that life does get more complicated for your family when work arrangements shift. The changes may cause some stress for all involved, but this small price to pay will be worth it. We think you're going to experience a new level of engagement with your family after you return to work. So, even though you may not have as much total time together, the time you do share will be more vibrant and engaging.

To help alleviate some of the initial stress, you will need to prepare your kids for their new arrangements and ensure you have the support of your family. Without it, your transition back will feel significantly harder. Even if you have the best child care in the world, there are logistics to work out, business travel to schedule around, work events conflicting with school events. Oh, and when someone gets sick (not Mom), someone needs to pick up the slack (often Mom). So, what can help? Systems. That's what you need to make it work. Systems and a lot of communication.

Enjoy it, revel in how far you've come, and get ready to get to work.

Family Matters: Prepping Everyone for Your Return

When I planted the seed of going back to work, I wasn't nervous about talking to my husband about it, Jen says. He's known me since we were in law school and knew I struggled with being at home. He didn't want to see me have major regrets ten years down the road—he wanted me to be happy. I also didn't ask my kids if they were okay with the decision. Rather, I explained to them what it meant for them, me, and us as a family, and the changes that would happen. I talked about everyone's schedule: what my general hours would be; who would be driving them; if I would see them in the morning and at bedtime.

The fact of the matter is I don't see my kids that much less now. My middle and high school kids are off to school at 7:15 a.m. and home by dinnertime, so I'm not missing huge chunks of their day. Countless parents can tell you, asking your kids right after school, "How was your day?" or "What did you do in school today?" will garner a single-word response every single time: *fine*. We get it. Kids need time to decompress and process what happened at school. We do, too.

The best thing you can do is to be clear and direct with your kids about why you are going back to work, and to do so in positive terms. You think you could still be a great accountant and want to give it a try. Or that it's really important for boys and girls to know that they have to be able to support themselves.

It helped to share all of my emotions about returning with my kids, Jen says. It helped them feel a part of the process and become supportive of my ambitions, and it also made them my biggest cheerleaders. The truth is they were a big part of the reason that I was going to return to work an even better version of my former working self. I wanted to show my daughter Grace that it was important to have a career. Grace has been fortunate to grow up in a two-parent upper-middle-class household, and I worried she wouldn't have the same drive for financial independence that was ingrained in me at an early age. Growing up in a financially strained home was hugely motivating for me. The most important lessons are caught, not taught, and I wanted to show Grace that it's okay to work, that it's okay to have a family and still work. It's good to split up household chores. It's good to have some independence. That actually works quite nicely.

In a study of 50,000 adults in twenty-five countries, daughters of working mothers completed more years of education, were more likely to be employed and in supervisory roles, and earned higher incomes. In the United States, that same study revealed daughters of working mothers earned 23 percent more than daughters of stay-at-home mothers, after controlling for demographic factors. There are other hidden benefits, too. Stacey credits her mom's work as the reason she can throw a meal together really quickly: My mom would call and ask me to get dinner started so I learned how to make pork chops, stir fries, spaghetti—you name it!

Getting your family on board is crucial. Their encouragement and support is your best ally against getting stuck in place because of fear. When a woman returns to work, or takes on a different, more challenging role, little changes on the home front make the transition easier. Talk about these changes with your partner, too.

What will this mean for his or her schedule? If you're stepping into real estate, will you need to block your schedule for open house Sundays? What have you been doing for the family that you will no longer be able to? Dry-cleaning runs? Paying all the bills? How will you guys divide and conquer these tasks? Much like the communication lessons we laid out in Part 1, you will need to discuss your next chapter together.

We know it's hard to do but try to worry less about how your kids will adapt when you go back to work. Kids are resilient. Talk with them about your prior commitments and that you may not be able to volunteer quite as much at their school and perhaps discuss what you could do instead. In many ways, it's really good for kids to have a little more independence. And when they tell you they're really proud of you, it will make some of your worries go away.

Here's what else you need to do to get through the transition.

Finish up any work projects. If you're freelancing, begin to wrap up projects with your client. There may be a period of time where you're pulling double time, but know this is just temporary. You don't want to leave uncompleted work on the table. Transition volunteer roles, too. Do you have any big responsibilities right now? Try to find someone to take them on for you. You will want to focus on your new job and then figure out how much extra time you have to devote to volunteering.

Make spreadsheets and kid schedules. Organize car pools for all your kids' activities. Routine plus communication are a working parent's best allies. Your kids will feel less anxious if they know where you are and who is picking them up.

Learn to say no. Do not overcommit, especially in the first few months back. Ease back into your new work schedule and don't make things more difficult on yourself. Before you say yes to a volunteer gig or a social event, think about all the things that saying "yes" entails: Getting a babysitter, driving an hour, missing a meeting. If it's too much, don't be afraid to say no. There's a chapter in Shonda Rhimes's book, *Year of Yes*, entitled "Yes to No," in which she details the importance of saying yes to yourself, which often means having a difficult conversation to say no to someone else. It's really true—try to keep this in perspective when you decline that next invitation. And remember, "No" is a full sentence!

Make time for family dinner. We both take this time very seriously. Phones are turned off, and we are talking about our days. That has been key for our families. Yes, you may learn slightly more about what your kids are up to—or who they have a crush on—by eavesdropping on car-pool conversations. But having this nightly tradition is the secret to making it all work for us. Jen and her family always have a "fancy" dinner together at home on Friday nights. Everyone helps to prepare dinner and then they spend hours together eating, talking, and hearing about each other's weeks. So even if it is impossible to do family dinner every night (we get it!), try to at least dedicate a few nights a week to them. Put down the phone when you're home and turn off all notifications of incoming calls, emails, and texts. We have learned that all of those messages will be there when you return to your technology.

Make time for your friends. Not spending as much time with your friends will be a big change in your life. Your friends who you once saw daily at pickup or around town will feel like you've gone missing. Don't try to keep up with your old social schedule—something will have to give. Make a point to text with or call them on your commute, plan a group drinks outing, or maybe even start a book club or wine club or any excuse to get together every six weeks. Again, remember it is the quality time that counts.

Update your wardrobe. When was the last time you pulled out your old work wardrobe? If you've spent the last several years in your weekend wear, restocking work clothes is absolutely essential before you begin your new job. Styles have changed and you don't want to look like you're stuck in a style from a decade ago. Also, check out great companies like M.M.LaFleur or Rent the Runway, which make trying out a new work wardrobe easy.

Figure out your new schedule for personal stuff. Salon trips, drugstore shopping, manicures, exercising—the list goes on and on. Blocking time on your calendar for your personal to-dos seems to fall to the lowest priority when you have work and family obligations, but it is essential that you schedule them just as you would any other commitment. Yes, it's that important. Also, until you're acclimated to your new role and work culture, you're likely to come home a bit drained. Make a point to take a yoga glass or grab a coffee with a friend. Or just read a good book. You need to prioritize your own free time to stay balanced and avoid burnout.

Make child-care arrangements. Last, but definitely the most important task, is finding someone to take over your daytime (or early evening, depending on your circumstances) child-care responsibilities. Hiring a fantastic babysitter or after-school program can take time, but your first priority is making sure you have a trustworthy, reliable person watching your kids. Post a request on your town's Facebook page, or on sites like Care.com and UrbanSitter.com, ask sitters you have used if they're looking for after-school hours, see if your school has after-care programs, and put a posting at local colleges. Again, this can be a temporary solution until you find a more permanent one.

If your kids are now in full-day school, your child-care needs may change. If your kids are older, having someone cook, grocery shop, and help them with their homework may be more helpful than a traditional babysitter. Elizabeth Scott discovered that having someone who can have dinner on the table is the biggest stress relief of all. "It's the little things like that that are equally as important for women to succeed and be happy at work," she says. If that's not a financial possibility for you, try meal prep companies or batch cooking on Sundays.

Lynn Perkins, CEO and cofounder of UrbanSitter, says that 50 percent of people coming to their site are looking for that dynamo, consistent after-school sitter, who can do school pickup and activity drop-off. *And* shows up. Every day. You know, your doppelganger. Lynn says to think creatively for people who may fit the bill. First, ask around if there's a family with young children who has a full-time care provider but might be willing to give up afternoon hours. A person in a creative field, like an actress, artist, or musician, might have the freedom of a flexible schedule to work for you around their auditions and studio time. And, most common, local college sitters who have regular availability. The ideal scenario, Lynn says, is to find two college sitters who are friends because this type of role tends to see a shorter commitment—schedules change, full-time jobs happen. If you can divvy up the job into two days for one and three days for the other—to have a team of two people—they will be more able to cover for each other (and text each other to figure it out) and in return you will have less of a scramble to find last-minute coverage.

Some more tips from Lynn to ease your child-care worries:

Have a structured agreement. Set up expectations of schedule and vacation days, and be very clear. One of the biggest challenges Lynn hears about is families expecting their care provider to do laundry, but they never explicitly said so up front. Also, be clear with how and when you want your sitter to check in with you. Is it okay to take kids to the park? What about when one of your kids is going to a playdate at a house you don't know? Communication is everything and we think it's always best to write everything down and share it with your sitter so everyone is on the same page.

Do a run-through together. We are guessing there are a lot of moving pieces in your family's schedule: show them where school is, activities, grocery stores you like to go to. Also, be clear on the household rules with the kids. What are your policies on snacks, having friends over, screen time? The more you can empower this person to care for your kids like you would, the happier everyone will be. It is also important to communicate to the kids that your new sitter is in charge while you are at work!

Don't be afraid to give constructive feedback. We can't tell you how many senior, high-powered executives tell us they have no problem delivering tough feedback to their team, but when it comes to the babysitter, they cower. We get it—you don't want this person to take out any strong emotions on your children. They do hold a lot of cards. That said, it will only lead to resentment if you don't step in and say something if it's really bothering you. Lynn advises to carve out time once a quarter to check in with your care provider when the kids aren't around—whether it's a phone call or stepping outside for ten minutes. Turn the tables and first allow the sitter to give *you* feedback. Ask, is there anything we need to work on in regards to the kids' behavior? Anything else you need help with? By showing the open line for communication, you then in turn have a chance to also talk about what changes you would like to make so the household can run more smoothly.

In the end, having a happy, low-stress home will make you a better worker. If you're not having to put out a ton of fires or worried that your kids aren't getting good care, you can focus on crushing your new job.

What to Expect at the Office

The clock didn't stop when you left: company culture and workplace communication has most likely changed and you need to prepare yourself for the shock of reentry. This was even difficult for Elizabeth Scott, who always had two feet in the door. When she went to Yelp, they handed her a Mac, which was foreign to the former PC user. "I had to learn how they liked to work—no PowerPoint, everything in Google Docs—and adjust to a scrappy agile culture. And I never even stopped working!" You can look at this story either with the glass half empty (oh boy, then what's going to happen to me?) or with the glass half full (I shouldn't stress about it because technology is moving so fast for everyone). Before you start, ask HR or your new boss what programs and operating systems your team uses and get a head start on how to use them. It will relieve some first-day stress. Search for tutorials on YouTube or for other free classes on LinkedIn.

"The workforce is changing constantly and rapidly every

minute," says Lindsey Pollak, author of *The Remix: How to Lead and Succeed in the Multigenerational Workplace*. "A lot of the rules have changed. So whether you've been out five or fifteen years you might be surprised that some of the givens in the workplace are no longer true." This is the first time in history, says Pollak, that there are five generations in the workplace together, from the traditionalist generation like Warren Buffett to Gen Z just entering. According to Pollak's research, 38 percent of Americans work for a boss who is younger than they are. Here are tips on how to fit in.

Show respect for every single person. Don't make an assumption about one's seniority based on age. The workplace has become much more democratic and the youngest person in the room might be the most knowledgeable, says Pollak. That is a huge power shift. With technology, companies are in need of certain skills, so someone who has been in the office for five minutes but is an expert in X might be the most critical employee. This is actually a huge advantage for someone taking a break. You could possess these critical skills. Also, there is so much more movement and it is less common to be surrounded by people who have been at the company for twenty years.

Ask about workplace norms and communication styles. Observe the culture: do people tend to meet in person or chat over Slack? These are things that you tend to learn over time, but when you're coming in after a break, you might need to be more deliberate, says Pollak. Instead of guessing and wondering, Should I text/call/stop by my boss, just ask how he or she likes to communicate: Do you like meetings? How do you like to receive updates? If there's something urgent, how should I let you know?

Know this: communication preferences are not necessarily generational; if someone is younger than you, don't assume they only want to text. Also, in some corporate cultures it's totally appropriate to schedule a meeting on someone's calendar, while in others it's rude. If you're new, casually ask your boss or a colleague, What's the best way to schedule a meeting with you? Pollak recalls in her first job she would send formal business letters because that's what you did. Now you can text, email, Slack, message on Twitter. She has one client who only responds to DMs on Instagram. So you have to ask; no one is offended if you do.

When Jen started at her law firm, she had several "tech" tutorial sessions—all new employees were granted this, not just the ones who took a career break. Don't be shy; take advantage of opportunities like this and even ask the "teacher" to give you extra sessions if you feel you need them.

Be prepared for open floor plans. The office environment has become much more collaborative and transparent. You may be sitting in an open-plan workspace where boundaries are more fluid than the workplace you left. This means last-minute drop-bys to brainstorm a sales pitch, or a question lobbed over several cubicles. Your boss may not schedule weekly staff meetings, favoring an open-door policy to discuss any pressing issues in real time. There are some easy ways to deal with this—learn to keep conversations to a minimum and buy a pair of headphones. Your coworkers may also bounce around. DeskPlus, a flexibility term coined by the team at Werk, where employees are based out of a company office but can work at a location of their choosing for some portion of their time (that is, a common area, or from home), is the most sought after type of flexibility, with 84 percent of their survey respondents requesting it.

Drop the self-deprecation. As we advised in our interview tips, don't joke about your lack of knowledge or make it about your age. Once you're working again, people won't remember that you even had a gap. Don't be afraid to ask for help: most companies have people dedicated to helping new employees onboard. You're starting at a new company and it's only normal to have to figure out how to dress, act, and work. Speaking of, be sure to look around and see what other people are wearing. Your shift dresses may still be fashionable, but if everyone is wearing jeans and a T-shirt, you may have to adjust your wardrobe. Don't become someone you're not, but find the "you" version of the company's dress code. This advice goes for anyone—maybe you worked at GE your whole career and now you're at a start-up; the rules are different!

Above all, give yourself time to adjust. Do a good job, but don't try to prove yourself too hard out of the gate. Listen more than you talk. And know, change is hard. Don't throw in the towel just because you missed a parent-teacher conference or you sent a confidential email to the wrong person. It takes time to get back into your routine and prove yourself as a worker.

When It's Not Working Out

You also shouldn't feel like you're stuck and that you have to be at a job for a prescribed amount of time before you can move on. The loyalty era (you need to work at a company for two years to show that you're a reliable employee) has been overtaken by the gig economy. It's not unusual for people to change jobs every year. Know that every company has issues and the grass isn't always greener on the other side. You might find that you're regretting stepping into a full-time role, that it is difficult to manage at this point in your life so quickly, but before you make a rash decision, and similar to the advice in the beginning of the book, ask yourself, what is your biggest pain point? There's no reason you can't ask for flexibility or a change now even though you didn't when you got the offer.

And sometimes you know when you need to walk away.

Clara, an investment banker with kids ages nine, seven, and two, also returned to work through a re-entry program after taking a five-year break. She left as a managing director and came back as a vice president—a serious drop in hierarchy. At her midyear review her manager told her she was performing well, but that she needed to put in a little bit more face time with the other bankers—and to stop acting like a managing director (!). She was advised that she needed to stay later if others were staying late. This was not what Clara was told at her interview. She was told that performance, not politics, was the measurement of success and that it was a great place for working moms. On that, Clara calls BS. Now she is entertaining interviews at financial institutions that aren't holding on to unspoken, outdated rules.

Here's the good news: once you move on to your second job after a break, people won't even know you took one. "At my new office, people don't know I took thirteen years off!" says Jenna Bloomgarden, who was offered a full-time job at Morgan Stanley after a returnship program. "You don't wear a sign that says 'I took time off.'" Instead, you are simply a working parent again.

If You Don't Ask, the Answer Will Always Be No

The best advice we can possibly give to a working woman is this: ask for what you need to be successful in the office. If you don't advocate for yourself in a way that shows positive benefits for you and the company, you won't get what you need to thrive in the office and at home.

People, and women in particular, have great fear about asking for what they want. "Anytime you speak with supervisors and ask for something, it is scary," says Lauren, a fund-raising manager. "Maybe it is a woman thing or a mom thing, where we are afraid that work will think we can't juggle it. But I realized, and was lucky to have a positive experience the first time I had to ask, that if you don't advocate for yourself, you won't have what you need to be successful." We have to get past the fear. Yes, the answer won't always be in your favor. But you won't know until you ask. If you ask in the right way.

When I came back to the *Wall Street Journal* after maternity leave, the agreement was that I would work in a part-time capacity for up to nine months post–birth of the baby, Stacey says. That date came and went and I didn't say anything. Why would I? I kept on working part-time. Then, at around the year mark, my manager asked, "When are you going to come back full-time?" But I had settled into this part-time routine. I had made it through the growing pains and it was working, for me, for my family, and, seemingly, for my colleagues. My manager pushed until I knew I had no choice but to make my case to keep my part-time status.

Years ago Stacey had developed a signature five-bullet strategy for any negotiation so she used that format and put her thoughts down on paper. Bullet 1: The introduction line where you express gratitude for current situation ("I'm so grateful to be three days a week") and clearly state your ask (to keep my part-time schedule). Bullets 2–4: supporting points for why this is beneficial for you and the company and why it will be successful. This part is very important: companies aren't going to say yes just to be nice; they want to know how it's going to positively impact the bottom line.

Bullet 5: a closing line that restates the ask and your gratitude to them for considering it.

I was ready; I picked up the phone and went through the script, Stacey says. I stayed on message and was ready to walk away from my job if they couldn't make it work. I knew I wanted, no, I *needed* a part-time structure at this point in my life. It wasn't an idle threat. So I ended the call by saying, "I appreciate all the time you've given me to date. If this will not work for you, I totally understand and I will move on." My manager took a long pause, picked the phone up off speaker, and said, "Fine. I have three kids and I wish someone would have done this for me."

The takeaway: you will never know until you ask. It's been said a million times over, but it bears repeating because women as a whole are apprehensive and afraid to negotiate for themselves because they're afraid to be seen as pushy or bitchy or, worse, that they'll lose their job over it. And while there is truth to the fact that there are repercussions for "women pushing more overtly on their own behalf" or being perceived as "difficult to work with," writes Linda Babcock, professor of economics at the H. John Heinz III School of Public Policy and Management of Carnegie Mellon in *Women Don't Ask*, negotiating for what you need isn't what determines your overall reputation.

Women are more pessimistic about the outcomes of negotiating (and not without good reason) so they typically ask for and get less when they do negotiate—on average, 30 percent less than men. And 20 percent of adult women (22 million people) say they never negotiate at all, even though they often recognize negotiation as appropriate and even necessary, according to research done by Babcock. When asking for flexibility, they're afraid they're going to lose their job over it—or be deemed as someone who doesn't want to work (which we know couldn't be further from the truth).

We know enough about the corporate landscape to know that not all companies will agree to part-time work, or remote work, or any arrangement that's not the antiquated system we have in place. If that's the case, the bigger question to ask is: Is this the kind of company I even *want* to be working for? Be realistic about your environment and what's possible.

If there are flexible policies that you want to use, use them. When Stacey was on a panel, one of the women in the audience asked this question: "My company provides a flexible work structure, but I don't feel comfortable using it—what do you suggest I do?" Simple: take it. You're not standing up for yourself or helping other people who are too fearful to step up if you're not taking advantage of policies that are already in place to make life a little easier for you.

Deloitte found that both women and men had a difficult time being comfortable taking full parental leave. Those surveyed thought taking a long leave would jeopardize their position, and more than half (54 percent overall, 57 percent of men) thought they would be seen as less committed to work. We need to change this story. Asking for what you need and taking advantage of programs offered to you does not make you a bad employee.

Push for the Diversity of Senior Management

Catalyst released a study that dug into one particular aspect of emotional tax for multiracial professionals, both men and women: the state of being on guard and consciously preparing to deal with potential bias or discrimination. Nearly 60 percent of men and women expressed feeling a psychological burden resulting from feeling different from their colleagues because of either race or gender. Catalyst defines emotional tax as the combination of feeling different from peers at work because of gender, race, and/ or ethnicity and the associated effects on health, well-being, and ability to thrive at work. Spoiler: the effects were not good. Productivity and work happiness dipped for those experiencing an emotional tax and feeling like they didn't fit in at work.

When you climb the ladder, there are fewer women and people of color at the top. And if you're one of the only senior women at your company, there can be a heavy weight to break the ceiling, get more women on board, and carry the feminist banner on your shoulders. The feeling that if you were to quit, you would be just another statistic. That hefty responsibility can be tough to manage. But one way to get through it: mentorship. Mentorship can feel like another to-do and time drain, but it can also provide fulfillment and satisfaction you may never have considered.

Take steps to nurture new connections by joining professional networks related to your passions or build on old ones. Social media also can help you identify someone in your professional circle with whom you can develop a mentoring relationship. We all need mentors to bounce ideas off, give us perspective, and help us stay motivated.

The impact of role models (or the lack thereof) on your career choices cannot be underestimated. One woman said, "Looking back, I would have done things differently if I had had a strong female mentor when I was at my breaking point—someone who could look into the future for me because she had been there. But I didn't, and I decided to opt out."

The lack of female mentors or "real" models is often cited as a major barrier for success. In the tech sector, 41 percent of women working in tech eventually end up leaving the field (compared to just 17 percent of men). The tech industry is notoriously laden with gender bias against female entrepreneurs, flagrant harassment, and an impenetrable boys' club that Emily Chang wrote about in *Brotopia*. This leads to a lack of female mentors (cited by 48 percent of respondents in an ISACA survey) and lack of female role models in tech (42 percent). Marian Wright Edelman said, "You can't be what you can't see."

As a young lawyer, tired from juggling two kids and my career, I never thought to ask the senior women at my company for advice, Jen says. It's not like there was no one who I could relate to. There were a handful with kids I could have turned to to learn about their own experiences and how they made it work. But at the time I was too tired and singularly focused on just getting to work to look that far up for mentorship. Now, when I was deciding to make the career move back into law, during the interview process, I specifically asked for the opportunity to speak with other senior female leaders. They would be the reality check I needed.

Parenting more than prepares you for leadership. You have to put out fires, tame emotion, know when to prioritize and pick your battles, make quick decisions, and motivate and inspire the people around you. Will there be ups and downs? Yes. But toast yourself—you did the work to get here. It's what will make you an amazing working parent again, too. Welcome back.

EPILOGUE:
IT'S TIME TO STOP
SIDELINING WOMEN

At the time of writing this book, twenty thousand women and men led a walkout at Google to protest that the company had paid one of its senior executives (Andy Rubin) an exit package of $90 million as he was shown the door for multiple sexual harassment episodes. The walkout led to the company abandoning its policy of forced arbitration for discrimination claims, though the leaders of the walkout felt the changes fell short of their demands.

But the power of their collective voices couldn't be denied.

Gender diversity is on everyone's mind—whether it's equal pay, harassment in the workforce, or women in top-level executive positions. It's one of the biggest issues facing companies across virtually all sectors today, especially in mid- to senior-level positions, where women are woefully underrepresented.

There's an imperative for all of us to figure out how to make a career and motherhood work better together—to strive for and do better. We also need to consider new programs and new policies, including public policies, like paid leave, child care subsidies, and equal pay. The companies that figure this out first are going to win the war for the best talent. It may not be easy to implement some of these policies but it is definitely worth it in the long run. Companies with 30 percent women in senior leadership can add up to 6 percent profit to their bottom line compared to those without. We live in a competitive world and for the United States to keep up with the global economy, corporate America must figure out how to do better with women, who happen to be graduating with higher education degrees at greater rates than men.

The bigger challenge is that, in the eyes of corporate America, care is unpaid work that is either marginalized or completely ignored. For the future of work to work for women, we must start putting a premium on care and expecting, accepting, and valuing the fact that at some point women *and men* will need to integrate caring for family members into their work life.

And yes, bring men and all voices into the conversation, whether it's through brown bag lunches or formal conversations around diversity and inclusion. Research shows that diversity of perspectives, education, and backgrounds not only leads to smarter, more well-rounded and thoughtful business decisions, but is also good for the bottom line. Having female leaders and mentors in top roles can improve a company's ability to attract and recruit top talent, and to counsel the younger employees who may be at the cusp of their own pregnancy pause. They innovate more, and they outperform other companies with a more homogeneous makeup.

A reimagined more flexible work environment creates a sustainable and profitable workplace that will be a win–win for everyone. We urge companies to dig deep—do the hard work. Change and shine.

This Is Not the End

It is the end of this book but it is definitely not the end of your story or the collective story of women in the workplace. Change is actually just beginning. There is much work to do. While we do our part to encourage corporate America to move faster toward change, we urge women and men to use their voices—to choose the best companies to work for and to advocate for change. We urge *you* to use your seat at the table.

Can you make small changes for yourself that have the butterfly effect of helping other women? In what ways can you disrupt the norm and start to influence your own small changes? Does your company have a women's initiative group or will you start one? Can you launch an internal PR campaign to highlight working women doing awesome things? Are you a hiring manager and can you make tweaks to job descriptions or add how and where you source talent? Can you say yes to the next person who asks for flexibility?

Our hope is that you take away three important themes from this book:

1. **It is possible to achieve the life that you want—both in your career and as a mother.** You now know that this may not be easy and that corporate America still has a long way to go, but it is possible and you do have what it takes. Own your story.
2. **Women have to support one another.** We must stop judging each other. Whether you are on a break or have a hard-charging career, whether you took a break or did not, we are all on the road together.
3. **You are good enough.** It's time to stop wasting our much-needed energy on guilt and self-doubt. Take the time to invest in and believe in yourself. You are worth it.

We have spent years dissecting, researching, talking about, and examining these issues and have done our best to provide you with the information you need to forge ahead in your path with the confidence it takes to land that perfect role for you, whether that role is in your current workplace, with a new career, or within your own home.

We hear thousands of success stories. We know them intimately, both our own and from many of the women we have coached through the years.

We encourage you to visit apresgroup.com and join the community and the conversation. There, you will also find:

- Webinars and workshops hosted by career coaches who will help you polish your skills, discover what's next, and boost your confidence.
- Career coaches who can further help you find your path.
- Job postings from companies who want you to come back.

At Après, we are helping people have the strength to slowly open that career door again to find companies that want them; we are guiding them to start doing something to boost their confidence, raise their profile, and unleash all that work goodness inside; we are giving them the tools they need to ease the transition; we are showing them how to roll with the punches. And we are bringing corporations into the conversation to prove that this is a demographic no one should ignore.

The world is ready for a change—it is changing—and we are excited to have you be a part of it. We are committed to making corporate America better for women. Will you join us?

ACKNOWLEDGMENTS

When a mutual contact introduced us in 2016, we knew from the first phone call that we could do more together to help women find meaningful work that worked for them, while also helping companies achieve greater gender diversity. After that first phone call, we pushed to combine our companies quickly, which allowed us to begin thinking bigger and more broadly about how to combat the issues facing so many women both in and out of the workplace. It was only natural that we teamed up to write this book, which has been an amazing collaboration and one we are hopeful will inspire and prove useful to our readers.

We want to thank *all* the women who have joined us in our Après journey. Our community includes women from just about every imaginable background and each is on her own beautiful, unique path. Thank you for helping us build a strong, vibrant community. We also want to thank the women who agreed to be interviewed for this book because we know your stories created a touchstone for our readers and reassured us that this book is necessary. Some allowed us to quote their full names, while others requested anonymity, which proves how fraught discussions about ambition, childcare, and gender roles remain both at home and in the workplace.

We're completely indebted to our writing partner, Kathleen Harris, who we each met separately and who, incredibly, contributed to both Après and Maybrooks. After many years in editing and content strategy at *Real Simple* magazine and then Levo League, the career advice site for young millennial women, Kathleen played an integral role in launching Après—working with cofounders Jen and Niccole Kroll to create its content strategy and directing the tone of the site. Years before, while Kathleen was still at Levo, a mutual friend introduced her to Stacey as someone to feature on Maybrooks, where the focus was on finding flexible work structures. As a mother of three children (at the time under the age of five), Kathleen was head of content for a well-funded startup and navigating the career and motherhood journey. She was commuting from New Jersey into the city but had taken the bold step when negotiating a new job to work from home one day a week so she could have more time near her then six-month-old twins and two-year-old. Her ask empowered others at the company to ask as well, and eventually everyone in the office was given the option to work from home one day a week. Kathleen has been leading on behalf of women for many years, with an ability to focus on what matters with the seemingly perfect amount of seriousness and fun, which is evident on every page of this book. We're grateful for her collaboration, her commitment to the project, understanding of the material, and superb writing skills.

Amanda Schumacher, whose public relations prowess helped introduce Après to the world in 2016, has been a key advocate for the book since concept form, and a critical partner in bringing it to life beyond the covers. Amanda has lived the "Après life" since she opted out of her hard-charging, full-time career for more time at home with her husband and two daughters. She has always been an advocate for women's issues and, chances are the first time you heard about *Your Turn* was probably in part because of Amanda's efforts.

Stephanie Hitchcock, Hollis Heimboch, and Brian Perrin

at HarperCollins had us at "hello," and there was no doubt we would collaborate together on *Your Turn*. In our initial meeting, Stephanie, a young mother of two, told us how she used Après to find inspiration and guidance in her own career when she needed a bit more flexibility at work—an ask she took successfully to Hollis. Stephanie's passion for making work work for women shines through on every page of the book. But we wouldn't have met Stephanie, Hollis, and the team if it weren't for Mollie Glick and David Larabell at CAA (both working parents with young children), who saw the need for this book and brought it to market. Mollie and Dave's deep understanding of the topic gave us encouragement to push for this book and their quick wit and formidable knowledge about the publishing world keeps us on our toes.

We also want to thank our team at Après, who show up every day to work on behalf of women—be it talking to companies, developing new content for the site, or helping an individual take her first step back into the workforce—especially Fran Garvey, Amy Nidds, and Jordan Martindell. Niccole Kroll, who cofounded Après with Jen, is such an incredibly important factor in Après succeeding and has always brought her unique view, original ideas, and desire to help women in the workplace to the table. Thank you to Robert Tuchman for his early investment and ongoing guidance—he's a pretty great dad of two girls and simply wants the world to be a better place for women. Our web developer, Caxy Interactive, has been an integral part of our journey—thank you to Hannah Deason-Schroeder, Josh Schroeder, and Michael LaVista.

We're lucky to work with a team of extraordinary career, life, and executive coaches who have contributed to this book, including Johanna Beyer, Julie Houghton, Laurie Palau, Barri Wachter, Rosie Guagliardo, Laura Riordan, Jennifer Chow Bevan, and many others. Thank you to Sherry Delo, Stacey's mother, for being an early advocate for women advocating for themselves personally, professionally, and financially. Thank you to Cari Sommer, Theresa Long, Natalie Smith, Julianne Metzger, Lauren Solomon, and Dana Keiles for early reads, sounding boards, and on-point feedback. Jen would also like to thank Epstein Becker Green for creating a culture where female lawyers (many of whom also happen to be mothers) are supported and therefore able to succeed, both at work and at home.

Thank you to our families for their support and encouragement of this project: David Gefsky, Gabe Madway, Jack and Sherry Delo, and Carrice and Mark McKenna.

Finally, because we have never taken a large investment, we are grateful to the many companies we have worked with that have supported bringing women back into the workplace. There are too many to list here individually, but their efforts can be found throughout the Après website.

NOTES

Introduction

3   *There are 3.6 million women on the career sidelines:* Committee for Economic Development of the Conference Board, *Helping Skilled Workers Return to Work following a Career*, Arlington, VA: Committee for Economic Development, April 11, 2018, https://www.ced.org/reports/helping-skilled-workers-return-to-work-following-a-career-break.

3   *93 percent of those who have taken a career break:* Sylvia Ann Hewlett and Carolyn Buck Luce, "Off-Ramps and On-Ramps: Keeping Talented Women on the Road to Success," *Harvard Business Review*, March 1, 2005, https://hbr.org/2005/03/off-ramps-and-on-ramps-keeping-talented-women-on-the-road-to-success.

7   *Study after study shows that profitability increases:* R. D. Adler, "Women in the Executive Suite Correlate to High Profits," Pepperdine University, 2001, https://pdfs.semanticscholar.org/e5f3/025e7aae2ea096f5fe7cc63f2247183c80de.pdf.

7   *more women are graduating from college than men:* "Total Undergraduate Fall Enrollment in Degree-Granting Postsecondary Institutions, by Attendance Status, Sex of Student, and Control and Level of Institution: Selected Years, 1970 Through 2026," National Center for Education Statistics, 2017, https://nces.ed.gov/programs/digest/d16/tables/dt16_303.70.asp.

7   *Since 1962 there had been dramatic growth:* Alison Burke, "10

Facts About American Women in the Workforce," Brookings Institution, December 5, 2017, https://www.brookings.edu/blog/brookings-now/2017/12/05/10-facts-about-american-women-in-the-workforce.

8   *Approximately 26 percent:* Gregor Aisch, Josh Katz, and David Leonhardt, "Where Working Women Are Most Common," *New York Times*, January 6, 2015, https://www.nytimes.com/interactive/2015/01/06/upshot/where-working-women-are-most-common.html.

8   *Does it help to have a spouse:* Hannah Seligson, "The New 30-Something," *New York Times*, March 2, 2019, https://www.nytimes.com/2019/03/02/style/financial-independence-30s.html.

8   *The IMF and other think tanks:* Alison Burke, "10 Facts About American Women in the Workforce."

9   *the United States is the only first-world country:* Matthew Phillips, "Countries Without Paid Maternity Leave: Swaziland, Lesotho, Papua New Guinea and the United States of America," *Quartz*, January 15, 2014, https://qz.com/167163/countries-without-paid-maternity-leave-swaziland-lesotho-papua-new-guinea-and-the-united-states-of-america.

10   *Lyft, Starbucks, and Microsoft:* John Kell, "Starbucks Will Now Allow New Fathers to Take Paternity Leave," *Fortune*, January 19, 2017, http://fortune.com/2017/01/19/starbucks-paternity-maternity-leave, and Courtney Connley, "15 Great Companies for Parents," CNBC, September, 19, 2017, https://www.cnbc.com/2017/09/19/15-companies-with-generous-parental-leave-policies.html.

10   *New York passed a paid family leave law:* "New York State Paid Family Leave Act," New York City Bar, modified January 2019, https://www.nycbar.org/get-legal-help/article/employment-

and-labor/family-medical-leave-act-fmla/new-york-state-paid-family-leave-act.

11 *And research shows that after only one year:* "Mums on Maternity Leave Lack the Confidence to Return to Work," Association of Accounting Technicians, April 17, 2013, https://www.aat.org.uk/news/article/mums-on-maternity-leave-lack-confidence.

12 *There are more than 15 million:* Bureau of Labor Statistics, "Employment Characteristics of Families—2017," news release, April 19, 2018, https://www.bls.gov/news.release/pdf/famee.pdf.

Chapter 1: Welcome to the Messy Middle

20 *In 2012, the Pew Research Center:* Wendy Wang, Kim Parker, and Paul Taylor, *Breadwinner Moms* (Washington, DC: Pew Research Center, 2013), http://www.pewresearch.org/wp-content/uploads sites/3/2013/05/Breadwinner_moms_final.pdf.

20 *42 percent of mothers admitted to reducing their work hours:* Pew Research Center, *On Pay Gap, Millennial Women Near Parity—for Now* (Washington, DC: Pew Research Center, 2013), http://www.pewresearch.org/wp-content/uploads/sites/3/2013/12/gender-and-work_final.pdf.

20 *LeanIn McKinsey Women in the Workplace 2018 report found that 81 percent:* Alexis Krivkovich, Marie-Claude Nadeau, Kelsey Robinson, Nicole Robinson, Irina Starikova, and Lareina Yee, "Women in the Workplace 2018," McKinsey & Company, October 2018, https://www.mckinsey.com/featured-insights/gender-equality/women-in-the-workplace-2018.

20 *the Women in the Workplace Report also shows:* Krivkovich et al., "Women in the Workplace 2018."

21 *Indra Nooyi, PepsiCo's first female chief executive:* Marilyn Haigh, "Indra Nooyi Shared a Work Regret on Her Last Day

as PepsiCo CEO," CNBC, October 3, 2018, https://www.cnbc
.com/2018/10/03/indra-nooyi-shares-a-work-regret-on-her-
last-day-as-pepsico-ceo.html.

21   *wrote in a LinkedIn post, "If I'm being honest"*: Indra Nooyi, "Part-
ing Words as I Step Down as CEO," *LinkedIn Pulse*, October 2, 2018,
https://www.linkedin.com/pulse/parting-words-i-step-down-ceo-
indra-nooyi.

22   *are surprised by the demands of motherhood:* Claire Cain Miller,
"The Costs of Motherhood Are Rising, and Catching Women Off
Guard," *New York Times*, August 17, 2018, https://www.nytimes
.com/2018/08/17/upshot/motherhood-rising-costs-surprise
.html.

22   *the median age of when women have their first child:* Nora
Caplan-Bricker, "For the First Time Ever, Thirty-Something
Women Are Having More Babies Than Their Twenty-Something
Counterparts," *Slate*, May 17, 2017, http://www.slate.com/blogs/
xx_factor/2017/05/17/cdc_data_says_women_in_their_thirties_
are_having_more_babies_than_women.html.

22   *and the number of U.S. women giving birth:* Gretchen Livingston
and Kristin Bialik, "6 Facts About U.S. Moms," Fact Tank, May
10, 2018, http://www.pewresearch.org/fact-tank/2018/05/10/
facts-about-u-s-mothers.

24   *In 2016 the Center for American Progress:* Leila Schochet, and
Rasheed Malik, "2 Million Parents Forced to Make Career Sacrifices Due to Problems with Child Care," Center for American
Progress, September 13, 2017, https://www.americanprogress
.org/issues/early-childhood/news/2017/09/13/438838/2-million-
parents-forced-make-career-sacrifices-due-problems-child-
care.

24   *70 percent of people who help care:* The National Alliance for
Caregiving, and the AARP Public Policy Institute, *Caregiving in
the U.S.: 2015 Report* (Arlington, VA: National Alliance for Care-

giving, June 2015), https://www.caregiving.org/wp-content/
uploads/2015/05/2015_CaregivingintheUS_Final-Report-
June-4_WEB.pdf.

24 *one in ten highly educated mothers decide to go:* Gretchen Livingston,
"Opting Out? About 10% of Highly Educated Moms Are Staying at
Home," Fact Tank, May 7, 2014, http://www.pewresearch.org/
fact-tank/2014/05/07/opting-out-about-10-of-highly-educated-
moms-are-staying-at-home.

24 *the most educated women in America:* Lisa Belkin, "The Opt-Out Revolution," *New York Times,* October 26, 2003, https://www.nytimes
.com/2003/10/26/magazine/the-opt-out-revolution.html.

25 *Many companies have made news for offering egg freezing:*
Sarah A. Donovan, "Paid Family Leave in the United States,"
R44835, Congressional Research Service, 2018, https://crsreports.
congress.gov/product/pdf/R/R44835.

25 *more than half of Americans don't use all their vacation days:* "State
of American Vacation 2018," U.S. Travel Association, https://
www.ustravel.org/research/state-american-vacation-2018.

26 *More than half answered they did:* Katrina Alcorn, "Do You Have
a Hospital Fantasy?" *HuffPost,* August 24, 2011, https://www
.huffpost.com/entry/do-you-have-a-hospital-fa_n_928559.

28 *millennials are quitting their jobs at a dramatic pace:* Deloitte
Touche Tohmatsu, "2018 Deloitte Millennial Survey: Millenni-
als Disappointed in Business, Unprepared for Industry 4.0," New
York: Deloitte Global, https://www2.deloitte.com/content/dam/
Deloitte/global/Documents/About-Deloitte/gx-2018-millennial-
survey-report.pdf.

29 *women are starting businesses at a rapid clip:* "Women Launching
1,200 New Businesses a Day, New Research Shows," American
Express, August 13, 2014, https://www.americanexpress.com/
en-us/business/trends-and-insights/articles/women-launching-
1200-new-businesses-a-day-new-research-shows.

29   *Middle-class life is now 30 percent more expensive:* Terry Gross, "'Squeezed' Explores Why America Is Getting Too Expensive for the Middle Class," *Fresh Air*, podcast, June 26, 2018, https://www.npr.org/2018/06/26/623367320/squeezed-explores-why-america-is-getting-too-expensive-for-the-middle-class.

29   *As Stacy Brown, founder of restaurant chain Chicken Salad Chick:* Guy Raz, "Chicken Salad Chick: Stacy Brown," *How I Built This with Guy Raz*, podcast, July 2, 2018, https://www.npr.org/2018/06/29/624713103/chicken-salad-chick-stacy-brown.

30   *In 2013, 37 percent of working mothers:* Pew Research Center, *Modern Parenthood* (Washington, DC: Pew Research Center, 2013), http://www.pewsocialtrends.org/wp-content/uploads/sites/3/2013/03/FINAL_modern_parenthood_03-2013.pdf.

31   *and the average age of retirement is sixty-six:* Emily Brandon, "The Ideal Retirement Age, and Why You Won't Retire Then," *U.S. News & World Report*, May 12, 2014, https://money.usnews.com/money/retirement/articles/2014/05/12/the-ideal-retirement-age-and-why-you-wont-retire-then.

Chapter 2: The Big Decision: Should I Stay or Should I Go?

34   *As do 10 percent of educated women:* Gretchen Livingston, "Opting Out? About 10% of Highly Educated Moms Are Staying at Home," Fact Tank, May 7, 2014, http://www.pewresearch.org/fact-tank/2014/05/07/opting-out-about-10-of-highly-educated-moms-are-staying-at-home.

35   *41 percent of Americans say they have a budget:* Hanscom Federal Credit Union, "How Many Americans Use a Budget?" Money-Wisdom blog, October 17, 2017, https://go.hfcu.org/blog/how-many-americans-use-a-budget.

36   *cleanings cost an average of $150:* "Cost Estimator Tool,"

Delta Dental, 2019, https://www.deltadental.com/us/en/cost-estimator.html.

37 *A sample calculation for a twenty-six-year-old woman:* "The Hidden Cost of a Failing Child Care System," web tool, Center for American Progress, 2016, https://interactives.americanprogress.org/childcarecosts, and Center for American Progress, "New CAP Calculator Reveals the Hidden, Lifetime Costs of the Child Care Crisis in the U.S.," news release, June 21, 2016, https://www.americanprogress.org/press/release/2016/06/21/139014/release-new-cap-calculator-reveals-the-hidden-lifetime-costs-of-the-child-care-crisis-in-the-u-s.

38 *birth rate just dropped to the lowest since 1987:* "US Birth Rates Drop to Lowest Since 1987," BBC World News, May 17, 2018, https://www.bbc.com/news/world-us-canada-44151642.

38 *steady increase in the cost of living since 1998:* "How Does the Current Cost of Living Compare to 20 Years Ago?" Investopedia, February 10, 2019, https://www.investopedia.com/ask/answers/101314/what-does-current-cost-living-compare-20-years-ago.asp.

38 *Portugal and Singapore have seen a steady decline:* Max Roser, "Fertility Rate," Our World in Data, December 2, 2017, https://ourworldindata.org/fertility-rate.

38 *Chinese residents are still having only one kid:* Leta Hong Fincher, "China Dropped Its One-Child Policy. So Why Aren't Chinese Women Having More Babies?" *New York Times,* February 20, 2018, https://www.nytimes.com/2018/02/20/opinion/china-women-birthrate-rights.html.

38 *Sweden, which is known for its generous family policies:* "Swedes Are Europe's Third Best Baby-makers," *Local Sweden,* March 16, 2016, https://www.thelocal.se/20160316/swedes-are-europes-third-best-baby-makers.

39   *breadwinner (42 percent of all working women):* Shawn M. Carter, "More Women are the Breadwinner at Home, but Most Still Say Men Treat Them Differently at Work," CNBC, March 23, 2018, https://www.cnbc.com/2018/03/23/more-women-are-breadwinners-but-are-still-treated-differently-at-work.html.

39   *Nearly a third (31 percent) of parents:* Patty Neighmond, "Poll: Cost of Child Care Causes Financial Stress for Many Families," *Morning Edition*, podcast, October 26, 2016, https://www.npr.org/sections/health-shots/2016/10/26/499166418/poll-cost-of-child-care-causes-financial-stress-for-many-families.

39   *D.C. also offers free pre-K for three-year-olds:* "Early Learning," District of Columbia Public Schools, https://dcps.dc.gov/ece.

40   *Universal Pre-K program:* Eliza Shapiro, "Bright Spot for N.Y.'s Struggling Schools: Pre-K," *New York Times*, January 1, 2019, https://www.nytimes.com/2019/01/01/nyregion/deblasio-pre-k-program-nyc.html.

43   *51 million, or one in six Americans:* "Asian Americans More Likely to Have Multigenerational Households," NBC News, August 25, 2014, https://www.nbcnews.com/news/asian-america/asian-americans-more-likely-have-multigenerational-households-n181191.

43   *The average adult lives only eighteen miles:* Quoctrung Bui and Claire Cain Miller, "The Typical American Lives Only 18 Miles from Mom," *New York Times*, December 23, 2015, https://www.nytimes.com/interactive/2015/12/24/upshot/24up-family.html.

45   Working Mother *magazine's Best 100:* "2018 Working Mother 100 Best Companies: The List," *Working Mother*, October/November 2018, https://www.workingmother.com/sites/workingmother.com/files/attachments/2018/09/wmm-100best-list-2018.pdf.

45   *California passed a new law that requires publicly traded companies:* Laurel Wamsley, "California Becomes 1st State to Require Women on Corporate Boards," National Public Radio, October 1, 2018,

https://www.npr.org/2018/10/01/653318005california-becomes-1st-state-to-require-women-on-corporate-boards.

45 *Women spoke of widespread sexism:* Liza Mundy, "Why Is Silicon Valley So Awful to Women?" *Atlantic*, April 2017, https://www.theatlantic.com/magazine/archive/2017/04/why-is-silicon-valley-so-awful-to-women/517788.

45 *report from the Center for Talent Innovation:* Sylvia Ann Hewlett and Laura Sherbin, "Athena Factor 2.0: Accelerating Female Talent in Science, Engineering & Technology," Center for Talent Innovation, 2014, https://www.talentinnovation.org/_private/assets/Athena-2-Infographic-CTI.pdf.

46 *led to "higher feelings of balance and job satisfaction":* Ines Wichert, "How Flexible Working Is Good for You—and for Your Career," *Guardian*, April 24, 2014, https://www.theguardian.com/women-in-leadership/2014/apr/24/flexible-working-career-progression-work-life-balance.

46 *It's also the number one search criteria for women looking for a new role:* Aoife Flood, "Winning the Fight for Female Talent: How to Gain the Diversity Edge Through Inclusive Recruitment," PricewaterhouseCoopers, March 2017, https://www.pwc.com/gx/en/about/diversity/iwd/iwd-female-talent-report-web.pdf.

46 *70 percent would have stayed if they had access to flexibility:* Tanya Byker, "The Opt-Out Continuation: Education, Work, and Motherhood from 1984 to 2012," *Russell Sage Foundation Journal of the Social Sciences* 2, no. 4 (2016): 34–70, https://doi.org/10.7758/RSF.2016.2.4.02.

47 *Employed mothers are nearly five times more likely:* U.S. Department of Labor, Women's Bureau, *Working Mothers Issue Brief* (Washington, DC: U.S. Department of Labor, June 2016), https://www.flhealthvalue.org/uploads/Projects/Babies%20Business%20and%20the%20Bottom%20Line%202017/Motherhood-In-America%20Report.pdf.

49   *What Warner found:* Judith Warner, "The Opt-Out Generation Wants Back In," *New York Times*, August 7, 2013, https://www.nytimes.com/2013/08/11/magazine/the-opt-out-generation-wants-back-in.html.

50   *guaranteed a job placement for up to four years:* United Federation of Teachers, "Paid Parental Leave," http://www.uft.org/our-rights/leaves.

53   Eleanor Roosevelt famously said: Dale Carnegie, *How to Stop Worrying and Start Living* (New York: Simon & Schuster, 1948), 187.

54   *Google says the number of new mothers who quit:* Alice Truong, "When Google Increased Paid Maternity Leave, the Rate at Which New Mothers Quit Dropped 50%," *Quartz*, January 28, 2016, https://qz.com/604723/when-google-increased-paid-maternity-leave-the-rate-at-which-new-mothers-quit-dropped-50.

54   *Eighty-six percent of women:* Gretchen Livingston, *They're Waiting Longer, but U.S. Women Today More Likely to Have Children Than a Decade Ago* (Washington, DC: Pew Research Center, 2018), http://www.pewsocialtrends.org/wp-content/uploads/sites/3/2018/01/Pew-Motherhood-report-FINAL.pdf.

54   *All twenty of the largest companies:* Claire Cain Miller, "Lowe's Joins Other Big Employers in Offering Paid Parental Leave," *New York Times*, February 1, 2018, https://www.nytimes.com/2018/02/01/upshot/lowes-joins-other-big-employers-in-offering-paid-parental-leave.html.

Chapter 3: The Case for Staying

57   *Henderson shared on LinkedIn:* Amy Henderson, "Why Mothering Makes Us Better at Work," *LinkedIn Pulse*, May 11, 2017, https://www.linkedin.com/pulse/why-mothering-makes-us-better-work-amy-henderson.

57   *"I knew I had to be better":* MTV, "Jennifer Lopez Accepts the

Video Vanguard Award | 2018 MTV Video Music Awards," video, *YouTube*, August 20, 2018, https://www.youtube.com/watch?v=u3ovWzY-1Zs.

58 *Harvard-reviewed study of hiring practices:* Shelley J. Correll, "Minimizing the Motherhood Penalty: What Works, What Doesn't and Why," presented at Gender and Work: Challenging Conventional Wisdom Research Symposium, Harvard Business School, Cambridge, MA, February 28, 2013.

59 *McGinn found that women whose moms:* Dina Gerdeman, "Kids of Working Moms Grow into Happy Adults," *HBS Working Knowledge*, July 16, 2018, https://hbswk.hbs.edu/item/kids-of-working-moms-grow-into-happy-adults.

60 *But if you've decided to return after leave:* "Motherhood in America: 2017 Report," Ovia Health, September 2017, http://flhcc.org/up-loads/Projects/Babies%20Business%20and%20the%20Bottom%20Line%202017/Motherhood-In-America%20Report.pdf.

61 *Teens want their parents to be flowerpots:* Sue Shellenbarger, "What Teens Need Most from Their Parents," *Wall Street Journal*, August 9, 2016, https://www.wsj.com/articles/what-teens-need-most-from-their-parents-1470765906.

62 *We have a natural inclination to avoid rejecting people:* Robin Young and Jeremy Hobson, "Why Is It So Hard to Say No?" *Here & Now*, podcast, March 31, 2014, https://www.wbur.org/hereandnow/2014/03/31/saying-no-psychology.

67 *Ruth Bader Ginsburg doesn't cook:* History.com editors, "Ruth Bader Ginsburg," A&E Television Networks, updated November 9, 2018, https://www.history.com/topics/womens-history/ruth-bader-ginsburg.

67 *RBG had a young daughter:* Melena Ryzik, "Bringing to Life the Ruth Bader Ginsburg Only Her Family Knows," *New York Times*, December 27, 2018, https://www.nytimes.com/2018/12/27/movies/on-the-basis-of-sex-ruth-bader-ginsburg.html.

70   *it takes the average worker twenty-six minutes:* U.S. Census Bureau, "Commuting Times, Median Rents and Language other than English Use in the Home on the Rise," news release, December 7, 2017, https://www.census.gov/newsroom/press-releases/2017/acs-5yr.html.

70   *two-thirds of employees reported feeling burned out:* Ben Wigert and Sangeeta Agrawal, "Employee Burnout, Part 1: The 5 Main Causes," Gallup, July 2018, https://www.gallup.com/workplace/237059/employee-burnout-part-main-causes.aspx.

72   *A 2017 Pew study shows that 43 percent:* Gretchen Livingston and Kristin Bialik, "6 Facts About U.S. Moms," Fact Tank, May 10, 2018, http://www.pewresearch.org/fact-tank/2018/05/10/facts-about-u-s-mothers.

74   *About half (52 percent):* Pew Research Center, *Parenting in America* (Washington, DC: Pew Research Center, 2015), http://www.pewresearch.org/wp-content/uploads/sites/3/2015/12/2015-12-17_parenting-in-america_FINAL.pdf.

74   *Sixty-two percent of working mothers:* Care.com, "Care.com Survey Finds One in Four Working Moms Cry Alone at Least Once a Week," news release, October 23, 2014, https://www.care.com/press-release-carecom-finds-1-in-4-moms-cry-alone-once-a-week-p1186-q49877680.html.

74   *61 percent of mothers with kids under the age of five:* C. S. Mott Children's Hospital, "Mom Shaming or Constructive Criticism? Perspectives of Mothers," *Mott Poll Report* 29, no. 3 (June 19, 2017), https://mottpoll.org/sites/default/files/documents/061917_criticizingmoms.pdf.

79   *Companies with greater gender diversity:* Global Leadership Forecast 2018, https://www.ddiworld.com/glf2018.

80   *Nike offers a full on-site day care:* Lisa McGreevy, "Oh, Baby! These 11 Companies Will Help You Pay for Child Care," *Penny Hoarder*, June 1, 2018, https://www.thepennyhoarder.com/life/

subsidized-child-care-benefits, and Amy Elisa Jackson, "8 Companies with Onsite Childcare Hiring Now," Glassdoor blog, September 25, 2018, https://www.glassdoor.com/blog/companies-with-onsite-childcare.

80 *offer some level of concierge service:* Ben Geier, "These 32 Companies Have Concierge Services for Employees," *Fortune,* March 28, 2016, http://fortune.com/2016/03/28/these-32-companies-have-concierge-services-for-employees.

Chapter 4: The Case for Taking a Break

82 *A 2017 Brookings Institution report:* Sandra E. Black, Diane Whitmore Schanzenbach, and Audrey Breitwieser, "The Recent Decline in Women's Labor Force Participation," The Hamilton Project, October 2017, https://www.brookings.edu/wp-content/uploads/2017/10/es_10192017_decline_womens_labor_force_participation_blackschanzenbach.pdf.

86 *Forty-two percent of married millennials and 37 percent:* Robin J. Ely, Pamela Stone, Laurie Shannon, and Colleen Ammerman, "Life & Leadership After HBS Findings," Harvard Business School, May 2015, https://www.hbs.edu/women50/docs/L_and_L_Survey_2Findings_13final.pdf.

96 *About half of American women say they have no time for themselves:* "How Do Women Spend Their Time?" Real Simple, November 1, 2011, https://www.realsimple.com/work-life/life-strategies/time-management/spend-time.

96 *when tennis star Serena Williams's daughter Alexis:* Soraya Nadia McDonald, "Serena Williams Compares Being a New Mom to Being on a Plunging Airplane," Undefeated, August 22, 2018, https://theundefeated.com/features/serena-williams-compares-being-a-new-mom-to-being-on-a-plunging-airplane/.

97 *more than 45 percent of women:* "How Do Women Spend Their

Time?" Real Simple, November 1, 2011, https://www.realsimple
.com/work-life/life-strategies/time-management/spend-time.

100 *The National At-Home Dad Network:* "Statistics on Stay-at-Home
Dads," National Stay-at-Home Dad Network, accessed March 18,
2019, http://athomedad.org/media-resources/statistics/.

102 *Studies have also shown that having kids do chores:* K. J. Dell'An-
tonia, "Happy Children Do Chores," *New York Times,* August
18, 2018, https://www.nytimes.com/2018/08/18/opinion/sunday/
children-chores-parenting.html.

103 *Nora Ephron was fifty-one:* Biography.com editors, "Nora Ephron Biography," A&E Television Networks, November 9, 2015,
https://www.biography.com/people/nora-ephron-212142.

103 *Nancy Meyers was forty-eight:* Suzy Evans, "Tribeca: Nancy
Meyers Talks Signature Look of Films, Attributes Long Career to
'Strong Will,'" *Hollywood Reporter,* April 26, 2018, https://www
.hollywoodreporter.com/news/nancy-meyers-talks-signature-
look-films-attributes-long-career-strong-will-tribeca-film-
festival-201–1106005.

104 *Many companies like Netflix, Etsy, Spotify:* "Paid Maternity Leave:
180 Companies Who Offer the Most Paid Leave," Fairy God Boss,
accessed March 18, 2019, https://fairygodboss.com/articles/paid-
maternity-leave-companies-who-offer-the-most-paid-leave.

105 *when roughly 80 percent of jobs aren't publicly advertised:* Dennis
Nishi, "Take Your Search for a Job Offline," *Wall Street Journal,*
March 24, 2013, https://www.wsj.com/articles/SB100014241278
87323869604578368733437346820.

Chapter 5: The Case for Freelance, Flexibility, and Part-Time Options

114 *Nurses, for instance:* "Nursing CE Requirements by State," Nurse
.com, https://www.nurse.com/state-nurse-ce-requirements.

114   *In California you need to register every year:* "California Lawyer Professional Licensing Guide," Upwardly Global, accessed March 18, 2019, https://www.upwardlyglobal.org/get-hired/california-professional-licensing-guides/california-lawyer-professional-licensing-guide/.

114   *By 2020, an Intuit study estimates:* Intuit, "Intuit Forecast: 7.6 Million People in On-Demand Economy by 2020," news release, August 13, 2015, https://investors.intuit.com/press-releases/press-release-details/2015/Intuit-Forecast-76-Million-People-in-On-Demand-Economy-by-2020/.

116   *nearly half of high-earning working parents:* Laura Vanderkam, "The Post-Bedtime Ritual of Successful Working Parents," *Fast Company,* November 14, 2014, https://www.fastcompany.com/3038542/the-post-bedtime-ritual-of-successful-working-parents.

117   *Social science shows us it can take twenty-three minutes:* Rachel Emma Silverman, "Workplace Distractions: Here's Why You Won't Finish This Article," *Wall Street Journal,* December 11, 2012, https://www.wsj.com/articles/SB10001424127887324339204578173252223022388.

117   *In the 1990s, researcher John Jost:* Stanford GSB Staff, "John Jost: Women Undervalue Themselves in Setting Pay Rates," *Insights by Stanford Business,* August 1, 1998, https://www.gsb.stanford.edu/insights/john-jost-women-undervalue-themselves-setting-pay-rates.

118   *Linda Babcock, professor of economics:* Katty Kay and Claire Shipman, "The Confidence Gap," *Atlantic,* May 2014, https://www.theatlantic.com/magazine/archive/2014/05/the-confidence-gap/359815/.

118   *"Almost half of Americans say":* Paul B. Brown, "The High Cost of Not Talking About Money," *New York Times,* October 12, 2017, https://www.nytimes.com/2017/10/12/business/mutfund/money-the-last-taboo.html.

121   *Pew research data found that 46 percent:* Kim Parker, "Women More than Men Adjust Their Careers for Family Life," Fact Tank, October 1, 2015, http://www.pewresearch.org/fact-tank/ 2015/10/01/women-more-than-men-adjust-their-careers-for-family-life.

124   *Harvard economics professor Claudia Goldin:* Claudia Goldin and Lawrence F. Katz, "The Most Egalitarian of All Professions: Pharmacy and the Evolution of a Family-Friendly Occupation," National Bureau of Economic Research, no. w18410, 2012, https://www.nber.org/papers/w18410.pdf.

Chapter 6: Getting Clear on What You Want to Do So You Can Go Do It

134   *According to LinkedIn, nearly half:* Blair Decembrele, "Nearly a Third of U.S. Professionals Are Career Sleepwalking: A Career Pivot Could Be Your Wake Up Call," LinkedIn Official Blog, August 15, 2018, https://blog.linkedin.com/2018/august/15/ nearly-a-third-of-u-s-professionals-are-career-sleepwalking-career-pivot.

137   *More than 50 percent of millennials:* Cliff Zukin and Mark Szeltner, "Talent Report: What Workers Want in 2012," NetImpact, May 2012, https://netimpact.org/sites/default/files/documents/ what-workers-want-2012.pdf.

137   *94 percent want to use their skills for a good cause:* Sara Horowitz, "94 Percent of Millennials Want to Use Their Skills for Good," *HuffPost,* December 6, 2017, https://www.huffingtonpost .com/sara-horowitz/94-of-millennials-want-to_b_5618309. html.

137   *The Deloitte millennial survey of 2016:* Deloitte Touche Tohmatsu, *The 2016 Deloitte Millennial Survey: Winning Over the Next*

Generation of Leaders, New York: Deloitte Global, https://www2
.deloitte.com/content/dam/Deloitte/global/Documents/
About-Deloitte/gx-millenial-survey-2016-exec-summary.pdf.

140 *Costs can vary from one hundred to several:* Christina Hillman,
"Back to Work with the Help of a Coach," Après, https://apres
group.com/back-work-help-coach/.

146 *According to the National Association of Realtors:* "Infographic:
Top Reasons for Choosing a Career in Real Estate," National Association of Realtors, accessed March 18, 2019, https://www.nar
.realtor/infographics/infographic-top-reasons-for-choosing-a-
career-in-real-estate.

147 *average school master's program:* "The Cost of a Master's Degree: 8 Drivers Within Your Control," Franklin University Back
to College blog, accessed March 18, 2019, https://www.franklin
.edu/blog/how-much-does-a-masters-degree-cost.

148 *In 2008, Goldman Sachs trademarked the term:* Carol Fishman
Cohen, "The 40-Year-Old Intern," *Harvard Business Review*,
November 2012, https://hbr.org/2012/11/the-40-year-old-intern.

148 *But even hospitals, nonprofits:* "Drexel University, Physician
Refresher/Re-EntryProgram,https://drexel.edu/medicine/academics/
continuing-education/physician-refresher-re-entry-program/.

148 *PricewaterhouseCoopers notes that 28 percent:* Pricewaterhouse-
Coopers, "Focus on Diversity and Career Progression Key to
Winning the Fight for Female Talent," news release, March
8, 2017, https://www.pwc.com/ca/en/media/release/focus-on-
diversity-and-career-progression-key-to-winning-the-fight-for-
female-talent.html.

150 *In this country, women own 12.3 million businesses—40 percent
overall:* American Express, "Number of Women-Owned Businesses Increased Nearly 3,000% since 1972, according to New
Research," news release, August 21, 2018, https://about.american

express.com/press-release/research-insights/number-women-owned-businesses-increased-nearly-3000-1972-according.

154 *For example, the Pennsylvania Conference for Women:* "About the Pennsylvania Conference for Women," Pennsylvania Conference for Women, accessed March 18, 2019, https://www.paconferenceforwomen.org/about/.

Chapter 7: The Habits of Confident Returnees

156 *In 2014, nearly 75 percent:* Janell Ross, "Most Americans Think Mothers Shouldn't Work Full-time. The Reality Is Far Different," *Washington Post,* October 15, 2015, https://www.washingtonpost.com/news/the-fix/wp/2015/10/15/most-americans-think-mothers-shouldnt-work-full-time-the-reality-is-far-different.

156 *The Center for Economic Development:* Committee for Economic Development of the Conference Board, *Helping Skilled Workers Return to Work following a Career,* Arlington, VA: Committee for Economic Development, April 11, 2018, https://www.ced.org/reports/helping-skilled-workers-return-to-work-following-a-career-break.

159 *one report says to expect:* Alison Doyle, "How Long Does It Take to Find a Job?" Balance Careers, September 6, 2018, https://www.thebalancecareers.com/how-long-does-it-take-to-find-a-job-2064245.

159 *Alice Walker famously said:* William Martin, *The Best Liberal Quotes Ever: Why the Left Is Right* (Naperville, IL: Sourcebooks), 173.

160 *nearly 90 percent of women who leave the workforce want to return:* Brigid Schulte, "Programs to Help Women Relaunch Careers Plummeted During Recession," *Washington Post,* October 17, 2014, https://www.washingtonpost.com/news/local/

wp/2014/10/17/back-to-work-women-whove-opted-out-face-stigma-struggle-to-get-back-in/.

162   *Nancy Pelosi:* "Nancy Pelosi Biography," *Encyclopedia of World Biography,* accessed March 18, 2019, https://www.notablebiographies .com/news/Ow-Sh/Pelosi-Nancy.html.

162   *She told* Politico, *"It is really an opportunity"*: "Nancy Pelosi Remembers 'Get a Life' Moment," video, *Politico,* December 4, 2013, https://www.politico.com/video/2013/12/nancy-pelosi-remembers-get-a-life-moment-004963.

164   *"As she made the beds"*: Betty Friedan, *The Feminine Mystique* (New York: Norton, 1963).

166   *Statistics show that women:* Tara Sophia Mohr, "Why Women Don't Apply for Jobs Unless They're 100% Qualified," *Harvard Business Review,* August 25, 2014, https://hbr.org/2014/08/why-women-dont-apply-for-jobs-unless-theyre-100-qualified.

167   *A 2013 British study found that women on maternity leave:* "Mums on Maternity Leave Lack the Confidence to Return to Work," Association of Accounting Technicians, April 17, 2013, https:// www.aat.org.uk/news/article/mums-maternity-leave-lack-confidence-return-work.

169   *Research has shown that having an accountability partner:* Leigh Stringer, "Forget Mentors, Find an Accountability Partner," Quiet Revolution, accessed March 18, 2019, https://www.quietrev .com/forget-mentors-find-an-accountability-partner/.

169   *why couples who have a high number of attendees:* Andrew Francis-Tan and Hugo M. Mialon, "'A Diamond Is Forever' and Other Fairy Tales: The Relationship between Wedding Expenses and Marriage Duration," *Economic Inquiry* 53, no. 4 (October 2014), http://doi.org/10.1111/ecin.12206.

171   *Alissa Quart writes about the Motherhood Advantage:* Alissa Quart, "The Motherhood Advantage," *Slate,* June 26, 2018,

https://slate.com/human-interest/2018/06/the-motherhood-advantage-the-evidence-suggests-that-becoming-a-mother-makes-women-better-not-worse-at-work.html.

172 *Studies found that opt-out women came back:* Judith Warner, "The Opt-Out Generation Wants Back In," *New York Times*, August 7, 2013, https://www.nytimes.com/2013/08/11/magazine/the-opt-out-generation-wants-back-in.html.

173 *AARP says two-thirds of adults:* Patricia Reaney, "Ageism in U.S. Workplace: A Persistent Problem Unlikely to Go Away," Reuters, October 19, 2015, https://www.reuters.com/article/us-employment-discrimination-age/ageism-in-u-s-workplace-a-persistent-problem-unlikely-to-go-away-idUSKCN0SD1Z720151019#w6RJVCWD4sIgP8dE.97.

173 *The average rejection rate:* Jacquelyn Smith, "7 Things You Probably Didn't Know About Your Job Search," *Forbes*, April 17, 2013, https://www.forbes.com/sites/jacquelynsmith/2013/04/17/7-things-you-probably-didnt-know-about-your-job-search/.

174 *Stay-at-home moms are half as likely to get a job interview:* Kate Weisshaar, "Stay-at-Home Moms Are Half as Likely to Get a Job Interview as Moms Who Got Laid Off," *Harvard Business Review*, February 22, 2018, https://hbr.org/2018/02/stay-at-home-moms-are-half-as-likely-to-get-a-job-interview-as-moms-who-got-laid-off.

174 *In October 2018, LinkedIn reported 15 million active job listings:* Craig Smith, "22 Interesting LinkedIn Job Statistics: By the Numbers," DMR, December 7, 2018, https://expandedramblings.com/index.php/linkedin-job-statistics/.

174 *could lift the gross domestic product (GDP) by 5 percent:* Binyamin Appelbaum, "To Lift Growth, Janet Yellen Says, Make It Easier for Women to Work," *New York Times*, May 5, 2017, https://www

.nytimes.com/2017/05/05/us/politics/to-lift-growth-janet-yellen-says-make-it-easier-for-women-to-work.html.

Chapter 8: Telling Your (Gap) Story

188   *was a major university research study:* Lauren Weber, "Why Young Women Play Down Their Career Goals Around Men," *Wall Street Journal*, January 24, 2017, https://www.wsj.com/articles/young-single-women-try-to-appear-less-ambitious-to-attract-a-mate-study-1485270001.

189   *A LinkedIn/Adler Group study found that 85 percent:* Lou Adler, "New Survey Reveals 85% of All Jobs Are Filled Via Networking," *LinkedIn Pulse*, February 29, 2016, https://www.linkedin.com/pulse/new-survey-reveals-85-all-jobs-filled-via-networking-lou-adler/.

191   *Harvard Business School professors:* Alison Wood Brooks and Leslie K. John, "The Surprising Power of Questions," *Harvard Business Review*, May/June 2018, https://hbr.org/2018/05/the-surprising-power-of-questions.

Chapter 9: Get in the Job Search Game

202   *In fact, 92 percent of Americans:* "Study Finds 92% of U.S. Adults Have Job Interview Anxiety," Anxiety.org, September 4, 2016, https://www.anxiety.org/adults-anxiety-job-interviews.

206   *If you've heard that 93 percent of communication:* Albert Mehrabian, *Silent Messages: Implicit Communication of Emotions and Attitudes* (Belmont, CA: Wadsworth, 1981), http://www.kaaj.com/psych/smorder.html.

210   *In her* Harvard Business Review *article, Priscilla Claman:* Priscilla Claman, "Choose Your Boss Wisely," *Harvard Business Review*, April 20, 2011, https://hbr.org/2011/04/choose-your-boss-wisely.

215 *there is a steady rise in the number of people:* U.S. Census Bureau, "2017 Data Release New and Notable," American Community Survey, February 7, 2019, https://www.census.gov/programs-surveys/acs/news/data-releases/2017/release.html.

215 *Research from Werk:* "The Future Is Flexible: The Importance of Flexibility in the Modern Workplace," Werk, accessed March 18, 2019, https://werk.co/research/the-future-is-flexible-werk-flexibility-study.

219 *One study of MBA students:* Deborah A. Small, Michele Gelfand, Linda Babcock, and Hilary Gettman, "Who Goes to the Bargaining Table? The Influence of Gender and Framing on the Initiation of Negotiation," *Journal of Personality and Social Psychology* 93, no. 4 (2007): 600–13, https:// doi.org/10.1037/ 0022–3514.93.4.600.

222 *women earn $0.78 cents for every dollar a man makes:* "America's Women and the Wage Gap," National Partnership for Women & Families, September 2018, http://www.nationalpartnership.org/ our-work/resources/workplace/fair-pay/americas-women-and-the-wage-gap.pdf.

223 *The subsequent equal pay initiative:* Bourree Lam, "The Two Women Who Kicked Off Salesforce's Company-Wide Salary Review," *Atlantic*, April 12, 2016, https://www.theatlantic .com/business/archive/2016/04/salesforce-seka-robbins/ 477912/.

223 *Buffer, a social media company:* Joel Gascoigne and Leo Widrich, "Introducing the New Buffer Salary Formula, Calculate-Your-Salary App and the Whole Team's New Salaries," Buffer Open blog, August 27, 2018, https://open.buffer.com/ transparent-salaries/.

223 *the National Partnership for Women & Families (NPWF):* "America's Women and the Wage Gap," National Partnership for Women & Families, September 2018, http://www.nationalpartnership

.org/our-work/resources/workplace/fair-pay/americas-women-and-the-wage-gap.pdf.

Chapter 10: How to Own Your Role as a Working Parent (Again)

227 *In a study of 50,000 adults in twenty-five countries:* Claire Cain Miller, "Mounting Evidence of Advantages for Children of Working Mothers," *New York Times*, May 15, 2015, https://www.nytimes.com/2015/05/17/upshot/mounting-evidence-of-some-advantages-for-children-of-working-mothers.html.

239 *And while there is truth to the fact:* Linda Babcock and Sara Laschever, *Women Don't Ask: The High Cost of Avoiding Negotiation—and Positive Strategies for Change* (New York: Bantam Books, 2017), 11.

240 *Deloitte found that both women and men:* Deloitte, "Deloitte Survey: Less Than Half of People Surveyed Feel Their Organization Helps Men Feel Comfortable Taking Parental Leave," PR Newswire, June 15, 2016, https://www.prnewswire.com/news-releases/deloitte-survey-less-than-half-of-people-surveyed-feel-their-organization-helps-men-feel-comfortable-taking-parental-leave-300284822.html.

240 *Catalyst released a study:* J. Travis Dnika, Jennifer Thorpe-Moscon, and Courtney McCluney, "Emotional Tax: How Black Women and Men Pay More at Work and How Leaders Can Take Action," Catalyst, October 11, 2016, https://www.catalyst.org/research/emotional-tax-how-black-women-and-men-pay-more-at-work-and-how-leaders-can-take-action/.

241 *In the tech sector, 41 percent of women:* Sylvia Ann Hewlett, Carolyn Buck Luce, Lisa J. Servon, Laura Sherbin, Peggy Shiller, Eytan Sosnovich, and Karen Sumberg, "The Athena Factor: Reversing the Brain Drain in Science, Engineering, and Technology," Center for Work-Life Policy, June 2008, http://scholarship.law

.berkeley.edu/cgi/viewcontent.cgi?filename=0&article=1009& context=bjell_symposia&type=additional.

242 *cited by 48 percent of respondents:* Sri Ravipati, "Report: Lack of Mentors, Female Role Models Top List of Barriers Facing Women in Tech," *Campus Technology*, March 6, 2017, https://campustechnology .com/articles/2017/03/06/report-lack-of-mentors-female-role- models-top-list-of-barriers-facing-women-in-tech.aspx.

242 *Marian Wright Edelman said, "You can't be what you can't see":* Tiffany Pham, *You Are a Mogul: How to Do the Impossible, Do It Yourself, and Do It Now* (New York: Simon & Schuster, 2018), 31.

Epilogue: It's Time to Stop Sidelining Women

244 *Companies with 30 percent women:* "Female Leaders Boost the Bottom Line," *Financial Times, September 26, 2017,* https://www .ft.com/content/f88a7c58-96ff-11e7-8c5c-c8d8fa6961bb.

INDEX

ABOUT THE AUTHORS

JENNIFER GEFSKY is the cofounder of Après, the digital platform that helps women return to the workforce after a career break and companies increase their gender diversity. Jen took a seven year career break and her experience inspired her to launch Après. Jennifer is also a partner at Epstein Becker & Green, a national law firm that specializes in labor and employment law. She lives in New York with her family.

STACEY DELO is CEO of Après, which acquired her workplace flexibility site Maybrooks in 2017. Stacey spent eight years as a multimedia reporter and producer with the *Wall Street Journal* digital network, where she went part time after having her first baby, and developed a passion in working to stop sidelining women talent. Stacey lives in San Francisco with her husband and two children.